The Fugitive Moment

From Hill Shepherd To Holy Calling

The Life Story of Rev. Ivan McElhinney

CONTENTS

FOREWORD

I count it a huge honour to be asked to write a Foreword to this book.

Rev Ivan McElhinney is a servant of God. It is that living relationship with Jesus which shines through these pages. As a fellow Methodist I am grateful to God for calling Ivan to ordained ministry in the Methodist Church for in that ministry he has offered gracious pastoral care, a powerful preaching ministry and wise leadership. I am personally thankful to God for Ivan, for he has been an encourager and a friend. My mind goes to an instance of which Ivan tells in this book where he, as President of the Methodist Church in Ireland, noticing my nervousness took time to pray with me in the middle of a busy auditorium, prompted by the Spirit. I know that many others could tell similar stories of how God used Ivan to point them to Jesus.

Rev Heather Morris

One of the book's introductory sentences says so much both about the book and about Ivan. It reads "As you read, reflect on your own story and give thanks to God for your journey through life". In these pages as Ivan tells his story he paints pictures with words; you will find yourself brought to Donegal fields, Belfast streets and to Caribbean boat journeys. Then at the end of each story comes a moment of reflection, a thought that stays with you, and all the more powerfully because of the tale which has just been told. More often than not those reflections point to God, whether that is God's goodness and provision in creation, the saving love of Jesus, or God's ongoing presence in the midst of times of grief and challenge.

This book will bring a smile to your face, you will enjoy this story. It will prompt you to think and it will be a blessing. My prayer echoes that of Ivan that as you enjoy his story, and that of Phyllis and their family, that it will prompt thankfulness to God for your journey through life.

Rev. Heather Morris

(Former President and now Secretary of the Methodist Church in Ireland)

TO MY GRANDCHILDREN

Layla, Honor, Marianne

Lily, Olivia

Owen and Ameyalli

GRATITUDE

My thanks to so many people who have helped me along the way and especially to those who assisted me in the preparation of this book: My wife Phyllis for her patience in the tedious task of typing. Mrs. Lynda Neilands for reading my handwritten draft and making helpful suggestions - all with such gracious encouragement. My son, Robert for his technical support in the field of digital technology - about which I know nothing!

As you read, reflect on your own story and give thanks to God for your journey through life. This project started during one lockdown, Hurricane Sandy in Jamaica, November 2012 and it was concluded in another lockdown - the Covid 19 Pandemic 2020/21.

First published August 2021

ISBN: 978 1838188931

CEDRIC WILSON

Designed & Published by Cedric Wilson
Email: cedricwilson@live.co.uk

PREFACE

It was the Autumn of the year 2009, and Phyllis and I had spent the night in my old Donegal home - the farm house on top of Ardnagesson hill. My mother Sadie, had passed away four months previously and as a family we had been removing valuables and precious items from the property. That process was now almost complete and we knew we would be the last people ever to sleep in that house. The water and electricity would now be disconnected as the century-old structure had so many hidden faults that it was fit only to be left derelict. After breakfast I took a rusty deckchair from the shed and placed it outside Granny's old garden hedge - exactly where a weathered wooden seat used to stand permanently in its place. My mind drifted back six decades to one of the vivid memories of my childhood - a moment when I had sat there before. It was the evening of the May Fair Day in Donegal Town. I knew that it was the May Fair because I had heard the adults all talking about it. There was a Fair Day in Donegal on the second Friday of every month but there was something very special about the May Fair. Something to do with the ending of the cold, dead bondage of Winter, the new life of Spring and the hoped-for glory of Summer. Cattle, sheep and all sorts of local livestock were sold at all the Fairs, and there were various stalls and entertainments in town and it was this social aspect of the Fair as an amusement show that peaked every year in May. From the vantage-point where I sat then and now, I could see across the valley to the next higher hill. Two roads were in view - the 'lower road' which runs up the far side of the valley, and the Copany road or 'upper road' which crosses the side of the opposite hill, rising from right to left until it disappears round a contour of that hill. Granny encouraged me to come and sit with her on 'the seat' and watch the people going home from the Fair. There was room on 'the seat' for two, so she sat with me for a while and then left me, quite contentedly on my own to observe the two roads. As there was no high hedge to obscure the 'lower road' I could see everything clearly and as the pace of the traffic was slow I had plenty of time to take in all that was passing along. A donkey and cart being driven empty home towards the mountain, a horse-drawn cart with a young calf, purchased in the Fair and tied in the cart, going to its new farm residence. A man with a short drovers stick guided two small store cattle and another with a longer 'shepherds crook' stick and a dog to heel, drove about a dozen sheep. Two old women, Maggie and Belle, from the far end of our townland lane, neighbours and life-long friends, simply walked along - one always a couple of yards ahead of the other - in their long shawls, treading their weary way home. Being so young I was not capable of much reflection and I'm sure that all I did at that time was note it in some deep way - I must have done that otherwise I would not have been able to remember it so vividly. But one thought that would never have crossed my mind then, was that the world on which I looked out that May Fair Day in (or about) 1950, would change almost beyond recognition by the time I would be in my teens or that such a varied destiny awaited me.

With Granny & Ade on the garden seat

Our life is a dream

Our time as a stream

Glides swiftly away

And the fugitive moment refuses to stay.

(Charles Wesley)

DONEGAL

I was born on 6th. July 1946 into the mid twentieth century post-war world. As usual for those days, I arrived in our farmhouse home built by my maternal grandfather, Bob Bustard when he married Jennie Reid early in the century. Bob's father had bought him the Ardnagesson farm to set him up on his own. Jennie brought a farm at Townlough half a mile away with her, which she inherited from her widowed Aunt Mary Wray - with whom Jennie had lived from the age of seven - and then Bob himself bought Slavins farm next door in Ardnagesson when it came on the market. It all sounds rather grand but the whole land holding only amounted to around forty acres.

My grandfather Bob Bustard (centre) & two helpers, spraying potatoes.

Bob was dead some years before I was born so I never knew him, but Jennie was one of my lifetime favourites. I loved Granny with her fulsome physique, intelligent mind and steady emotions. My mother, Sadie wasn't as tall as Granny, was very intelligent and would have been a professional had she benefited from a better education and unlike Granny she was for nearly all her life, very emotional and sentimental. I was to learn over time that this was her reaction to the bereavements of her formative years - the untimely deaths of her father and sister during the dark days of World War II, 1940/41. My father George, was a strong man in every way - physically, mentally and emotionally - my abiding memory of his strength is of his capacity to restrain young cattle that would have defeated a more delicate man - Dad could hold them without crush bars until the vet was finished!

My favourite uncle - Andy

In the 1950's there were seven residents of our home on the hill. Granny was the matriarchal head of the house and the actual owner of all the property. Dad and Mum worked hard, with limited resources to make ends meet, but through no fault of theirs, debt could not be avoided. The economy of de Valera's Ireland in the 1950's was comparable to that of England in the 'hungry 30s' and we were poor. But as we knew no rich people we had no resentment or jealousy over material things and we were happy. I was the oldest child and my brother Adrian (Ade) was less than two years younger. As brothers we went to school, worked on the farm, socialised and shared the same bed together for twenty years. Our personalities differed but we were very close. Charlotte came next - from an early age always alert to any trick her older brothers wanted to play on her! She was nobody's fool from day one. She won a much-coveted scholarship to Colaiste Mobhi, an Irish-speaking girls school in Dublin, and her academic life took off there - leading to a successful career in teaching. I was ten when Irene was born and I still think of her as the first child I helped to look after. As a result I have always had a special place in my heart for Irene as my kid sister.

Mum's emotional life was such that she found it utterly heartbreaking when any of us left home. Charlotte was the first to go - to board at Mobhi, and Mum wept for weeks. I'm sorry to record that for many years I underestimated Mum's sorrow and sense of loss in this regard. Near the end of Mum's life I was talking to her in Ardnagesson and I recalled that I got a letter from home soon after going to Cliff College saying that Auntie May had come to stay for a few days and I always wondered why. With a dark, sad look Mum said: "May was very much needed." Nothing more was said on the matter but I felt ashamed that only forty years later did I realise how very low my mother felt when I departed from the family home.

Apart from those who lived on the farm, the other branch of the family to whom we were particularly close was Mum's sister May and her family. Her husband, Andy Graham was a favourite uncle of mine from my childhood until his death. Their only child, Sadie has always been more like another sister than a cousin, this closeness lasting until the present time.

The kitchen was the hub of an ordinary country house like ours and there was an open-fire hearth in my early years. But the chimney of the house had a poor and unreliable draught and so it 'smoked.' This meant that when the wind blew from the wrong direction - which it frequently did - the kitchen filled with smoke. So Dad got a secondhand black stove, which solved the smoke problem but the downside was that the solid fuel had to be cut short to fit into the firebox of the stove. Pieces of firewood four feet long could easily be placed on a flat open fireplace but for the stove they had to be nine inches or so and not too thick. The family sat in the kitchen and when the neighbours dropped in they joined us there - just walking in unannounced and without knocking. Indeed if the door was ever knocked everybody sat up straight for it was sure to be the Guards (Police), the Minister or someone on official business! The one fire and source of heat was in the kitchen so it doubled as a living room and that was the place to be. There was another main room downstairs, the parlour - usually called simply 'the room' - with better quality furniture in it than the kitchen, but it was used so infrequently that I had the impression that you would need to be a visiting relative from America to sit on one of the nice chairs in 'the room!'

When you went 'rambling' to a neighbour's house you lifted the latch, walked on in, said "hello" and sat down by the fire in the kitchen. Any such formality as knocking and waiting to be admitted would have been taken as the height of snobbery. So my earliest memories are of our farmhouse kitchen; our daily living space where all the household cooking was done on the stove. Granny sat in her big,

With my siblings

My mother on Daisy

imposing armchair in the chimney corner as Mum and Dad came in and went out doing the many routine daily chores of a farm. In the Winter most of these tasks had to do with feeding the livestock, heating drinks for calves etc. Dogs and cats also inhabited the kitchen and occasionally other animals. A delicate new-born lamb or calf would be kept in the farm kitchen for a few days for life-saving warmth.

Fifteen yards away was the byre and stable. Our grey pony, Daisy lived in the stable and the cows in the byre. In my early days we had just three cows but later Dad built the dairy herd up to six cows - thought then to be milking in a big way!! The cows were milked by hand into a clean bucket - for such an operation you sat on a special small milking stool. Most of the milk was sent to the creamery and the calves whose births had started the flow of milk, were fed on the returned skimmed milk. The cream or butter-fat content was what the farmer was paid for. Sometimes we churned the milk in the kitchen ourselves - for which the milk had to be sour to allow the butter to separate from the buttermilk in the big wooden churn. It was worked with a beater up and down on a shaft protruding from a hole in the lid of the churn. Like so many farm jobs, churning was hard, sweaty work with two or three members of the family taking a turn at it. Mum had her clean wooden butter-pats to shape the fresh butter on a small board ready for use on the kitchen table - for the kitchen was a dining room as well as a cookhouse and living area.

Apart from a heifer being kept for a cow, we sold our calves off as store cattle at two years old, a big day out at the April Fair. We got up unusually early to round up the cattle for sale and walk them to the town. On the way we soon fell in with plenty of neighbours doing the same thing, so the road into Donegal Town was filled with groups of cattle being driven along, each by a couple of men and boys - all following close behind one another. My Dad or Granda Tom would send me on ahead to stand in an open gap into a field to prevent scattering and keep our stock on the road. When we got to the 'Cow Market', a scraggy open field above the town, all was chaos with hundreds of roaring cattle without pens. It was very difficult to keep your own beasts from running away and mixing with others.

Dealers moved around, inspecting the animals for sale. They would enquire about the asking price and then make a bid. It was all far from straightforward. There was a definite ritual to be followed with much running about, hand slapping, pretences of total lack of interest in the bid on the part of the selling farmer - pipe in mouth looking away from the dealer - enthusiastic intermediaries urging both parties to 'split the difference.' It was all a subculture in its own right, which disappeared suddenly with the introduction of cattle Marts in the 1960's. Then down on the Diamond in the town centre, there were young calves, pigs, foals and donkeys. You could see vendors and stall-holders with all kinds of goods - clothes, tools, crockery and dulce.

I remember a lively and deranged-looking calf getting out of control and running through a glassware display set out on a sheet on the ground, the high-pitched shriek of the vendor and the frantic effort of a couple of farmers wielding drovers sticks to regain the initiative! Of one thing I can be fully certain - the seller of glass got no compensation!

I was quite interested in cattle and I remember having a vivid dream that one of our cows was calving - always an awesome scene for a young lad. I woke up and sure enough a constant roaring was coming from the byre! I crept out of bed, slipped on my trousers and ran to see and the cow due to calve had done the deed. The poor newborn had staggered under the wrong cow, was trying to suck and getting kicked dangerously. I sprinted back to my Dad in bed and we both set about putting everything in order.

We once had a nice red shorthorn heifer due to give birth to her first calf. I was on my way home along the valley from our outlying Townlough Farm when I came across her just having calved a short time before. She had already licked the calf fairly dry so I put my head under the calf and carried it to the farmhouse. I proudly set it down in front of the kitchen window for Granny to see the new arrival - it's mother having followed me a quarter of a mile home. I didn't feel the slightest danger from her two sharp horns.

My favourite creatures of all were the sheep and the dog needed to herd and control them.

I saved enough small change to get my first ram lamb when I was eight or nine years old. The price of a horned mountain lamb, or 'scotch' lamb was only a little over £1 in the September or October Fair. In the 1950's you could at least double your money if the animal lived and thrived until it was one year old the following Spring. My dad's younger brother Uncle Tommy, bought and sold, helped and advised as he was a very good sheep farmer. I too became a sheep man on a small scale for ten years - eventually getting a few breeding ewes as well as the passing stock of 'scotch' lambs. It became known among some of the mountain shepherds

My sisters & cousin Sadie plus ducks!

A pair of draught horses

who knew Uncle Tommy, that I would accept orphan lambs and from time to time I was given them. I simply loved sheep and such a free offer was irresistible every time. One ram lamb I had was tied in the little field below the house all Summer, where he had an abundance of grass to eat and bottles of milk to suck every few hours. Mum quite rightly used to say that I was better at bringing these 'pet lambs' home than I was at feeding them! The trouble always was that as a pet lamb got older there was no hope of it staying out in the fields because it wasn't socialised with other sheep. This particular young ram was castrated to calm him down but he continued to make a dreadful nuisance of himself by hanging around the byre and farmyard. Our neighbour next door was the ageing widow of short stature Becky Wray and on a dark Winter's night when she was returning home on foot, my pet lamb, now fully grown, gave her a hard butt from the back. I must have been forgiven as I later became her grandson-in-law!

I was working with dad one day in the mountain bog, when I noticed some way off, a hill farmer with two dogs that were very good at controlling his flock of sheep. After a while he came to talk to my father and I could see that one of the dogs was female, a bitch, so I asked him for a pup. The following Spring word was left with my grandparents that John had a pup for me. The next Sunday I walked the three miles to John's house in the heather to collect a small bundle of black and brown fur and bring him home with me. I gave him the name "Shep" - from an Elvis Presley song - and he soon proved to be the best herding dog we would ever have on the Ardnagesson Farm. At four months old he started bringing the cows home for milking - his sign for that was when he saw Mum setting out the milking buckets. As soon as she started to fill the feeding vessels for the calves, Shep was off to get behind the calves and have them at the gate and ready for their meal. He gathered the wayward turkeys into their shelter every evening without fail. He was an absolute delight at handling sheep, he had all the right instincts and sense of balance and was in every way a truly wise and good sheepdog.

My paternal grandparents were Tom and Maggie McElhinney. They lived one mile away down the valley at Cully Crossroads and Uncle Tommy lived with them. Their home was a low cottage standing along the roadside with at least eighteen inches of thatch accumulated on the roof from the time it was built in the early 1600's until it was replaced by a modern bungalow in the 1960's. The fire burned continually on the hearth for all that time - being 'raked' with ashes covering the

Ewe & lambs

With my siblings & two pet lambs

The cows at the Lough to drink

Shep & my siblings

My parents at the farmhouse door in their latter years

Becky Wray

smouldering coals to preserve the embers overnight enabling it to be rekindled in the morning. The pots and pans for cooking were suspended from an iron crane with chains, enabling Grannie Maggie to adjust the height of the cooking vessel over the fire. By this fine-art method she baked delicious soda bread, boiled kettles and pots and prepared all daily food. The building was quite long and there was no back door, so any coming or going had to be done via the public roadside. The stable and byre were all under the same roof as the farmhouse and when staying at the house, I well remember, before going to sleep, hearing the horses snorting or stamping their feet. I very much enjoyed staying overnight in that house; there was an old-world picture-book atmosphere of mystery about the place which appealed to my imagination. There were strange, thick panes of glass in the little windows that seemed to be as old as the roof and Granny Maggie had a geranium plant that totally filled one window - leaning outwards towards the light.

That house never had electricity and the light in the kitchen was a simple wick oil lamp, small and basic, sitting oddly enough on an upturned bucket with cartoon characters painted on it. I had the impression that it must have started life as a beach bucket-and-spade sandcastle-making implement but how it ever came to be the lamp stand at the Crossroads Cottage I could never figure out. The cartoons, like the bucket, were upside-down but there it sat on the kitchen table, holding the lamp at the right height to cast its somewhat dim light all over the room. An old 'dresser' with its open shelves, stood against a wall displaying plates, bowls, mugs and jugs. Across the road, ten yards from the door, was a perfect spring well, with crystal-clear water constantly gushing up through limestone rocks through the driest of Summers.

One of my favourite people was Granda Tom. I would just hang about the farm with him and in the evening in front of the open fire he would smoke his pipe and continue to stimulate my mind by asking about all I was learning at school. He would talk about various aspects of farming life and tell old-time stories for hours. There was no interruption to the flow of conversation from radio or television. My grandparents kept abreast of current affairs by Granda sitting at the kitchen table reading aloud and slowly from a weekly newspaper. When I got into bed, I repeated after Granda Tom, one of those old nineteenth century hymns such as "Jesus tender Shepherd hear me" and I fell asleep as if in Heaven.

Uncle Tommy was then young, tall and handsome, had scores of sheep and a great working collie. There were always two good draught horses on that farm and I was always fascinated by them - they were so big and powerful and yet so well under control. A good day for me was a dry morning in the Summer when Granda Tom was going to mow a meadow with his two-horse mowing machine. There were so many chains to be hooked up to the horses' harness and then the two very long rope reins Granda used to drive and steer the horses. He turned the whole outfit, about eight yards long from the horses' heads to his seat at the back, to leave behind swathes of grass cut to precision. One year he had a new, young horse that had been 'broken-in' the previous Spring and he had already pulled the plough and the cart quite well but some trouble was expected with the mowing machine. The problem was the high level of noise, amounting to a considerable clatter made by the machine when in operation and the peculiar screech of the cogs when it was turning at the end of a swathe. The young horse towed the apparatus quite happily to the meadow, alongside his mature yokefellow - but what would happen when the blade was lowered for cutting? Dad and Uncle Tommy were on hand just in case and as it turned out, it was essential for them to be there. As soon as the machine began to work, the young horse squealed and reared up with one foot over the other horse's neck! At one point he lifted Tommy off the ground and it all looked as though he would never do this type of work but with some patient coaxing he soon realised that there was no threat and in half an hour he was doing the job peacefully. I got the feeling that Granda Tom had seen it all many times before and knew that all would be well. Dad made a journey to faraway Belfast to buy a used grey Ferguson tractor and that signalled the end of the era of draught horses on our small-holding farms.

Joey, the grey gelding, was one of Granda's last horses. He had a mild nature and I remember ploughing to plant carrots with him even after we already had the tractor. Jobs like that on a small plot of ground could conveniently be done with a horse even though their day was done in general terms. Ministers from a farming background recruited into the Methodist Ministry used to be called 'the boy behind the plough' and I like to think that in the literal sense, I may have been the last!

Our main crop was potatoes, usually alternated year-on-year with oats in the arable fields, and quite a bit of hard work had to be done with these crops - plus the hay and the 'turf.' For potatoes the ground had to be dug with spades if the planting method was 'ridges' or ploughed appropriately if the method was 'drills.' The seed potatoes were dropped by hand and covered with soil by spade in ridges, or by plough in drills. Cow manure had to be hauled by horse cart, or later tractor, from the 'doughal' to the planting ground and carefully spread where it was needed for the potato plants to grow fast. Needless to say, the dung stank to high heaven! The doughal was a manure pit at one end of a byre and there was usually a hole called a 'gowl' to facilitate the pitching of the cow-dung out of the byre on a daily basis. By springtime the doughal was piled high with dung ready to be used as fertiliser and it was ideal for potatoes. A little later, when the plants began to sprout and appear above the ground, the potatoes needed to be 'moulded' - that meant that some extra loose soil had to be applied to cover the developing tubers and prevent them from going green in the sunshine and spoiling. Throughout the summer growing season, fortnightly spraying to prevent blight had to be done - essential in dry conditions. Memories of the Potato Famine in the mid-nineteenth century, coupled with the occurrence of blight from time to time, meant that spraying was never neglected. The spray was a mixture of bluestone and washing soda, prepared in a large coopers wooden barrel and applied to the potato tops with a copper knapsack machine. The sprayer held around three gallons of fluid and was attached to the operator's back with straps. There was a rod for pumping with your left hand and with your right you directed the watery spray to the vegetation through a double nozzle. It was heavy when full and sore on the human back and then the nozzles could be blocked with particles and you had to blow them clear with your mouth. The spray mix was not poisonous but it had a nasty taste. Providing all these stages of growth were successful, and the spraying prevented blight, the crop would mature and be ready to dig - the early variety by June and the main type by October/November. On the old ridge system they had to be dug by spade and in the case of drills it was done by a horse-drawn spinner digging machine - much quicker and even more efficient when the tractor could power the process. There was plenty of work for boys as 'tatty-howkers' or gatherers of the dug-out spuds from the loose ground. This we did after school until it was pitch dark and all day on a Saturday.

It was usual for the fresh potatoes to be placed in pits and covered with rushes and a heavy coating of soil to keep out the winter frost and preserve them in the field where they grew, until the spring. It was a cold job down on your knees in March and April, lifting and sorting seed potatoes kept for planting and 'ware' or 'eating' potatoes to be sold if there was a market for them. Sometimes Dad used to load a half ton onto the tractor-trailer to sell door-to-door and to shops and cafes in Donegal Town and I tagged along as sales assistant! This taught me the skill of such sales and I started to take some vegetables of my own sideline production to the town by bicycle, to sell for pocket money. In this casual way I would sell small quantities of cabbage, carrots and early potatoes. On one occasion I wanted to see a particular John Wayne film and I had no money. But I had carrots in my own plot on the farm so I pulled about two stones of them, put them in a bag, balanced them on the handlebars of my old bicycle and rode the four miles into town. I knocked on the back door of the Abbey Hotel and the timid, unassuming figure of Dom Breslin appeared. I offered him the carrots, he weighed them and paid me a few shillings as a fair price. I bought a packet of roasted, salted peanuts in Rose Donion's little shop to eat during the film show and made my way up the hills home again feeling like a King! Dom Breslin never tried to cut a dash, or look the part of the successful businessman he was. His family owned the hotel, but Dom could be seen any day working alongside his staff doing any necessary work.

I never forgot him for enabling me to enjoy the cinema that night.

With oats, which we always called 'corn', we had less labour than with the potatoes. The field had to be ploughed and the soil refined with a harrow before sowing. This was usually fairly easy as potatoes would have broken up the ground the previous year. Dad's cousin Willie Wray, was the most skilled sower around and Dad always got him to sow our corn. With a special bag over his shoulder he knew exactly how far he needed to space his pacing lines up and down the field to spread the seed corn with precise evenness. As the young plants came up in bright green shoots, it was always obvious what a prefect job Willie had done in the sowing.

In a normal season, the corn took care of itself until Harvest in September when it was cut and bound by hand into sheaves. I can remember small patches of corn being cut by scythe but it was normally cut by horse-drawn mowing machine or later by the tractor. There was a special gate fixed to the mowing blade and an extra seat for the operator to offload the right amount of falling corn to be made into a sheaf. As a growing boy I counted it a great privilege to work the gate, using a peculiar short rake to push the crop away at the right intervals and the right quantity each time. A team of men and boys, and sometimes women as well, would follow the reaper making sheaves from the bundles left lying on the field. The sheaves were set up the day the corn was cut and bound into 'stooks' of three or four, to stand upright for withering and drying. This, like so many things, depended on the weather! The crows and wild wood pigeons were a hazard at this

Our terrier Spring with the family

Phyllis working at turf in the mountain bog

The thresher at work

Drumnahoul National School student body!

As a very young farmer I feed my hens

Horse at work in a potato field

stage and scarecrows would be set up in a field in a (usually vain) effort to keep them away. When the stooks were dry, the sheaves were built into a 'handshakin' or small ruck and thatched over at the top. Later still these solid rucks were dismantled and carted home to the farmyard to be built into huge corn stacks and carefully thatched with rushes, bound with ropes and sealed securely. The final and most exciting stage came in the Winter, when the big pink thresher came to whine for a few hours, powered by a belt attached to the tractor that brought it, to separate the grain from the straw. Our wee white fox-terrier dog Spring had a great time on threshing day, catching and killing rats, forced out of their comfortable abode so well stocked with an abundant food supply! He shook them so fast that they each died instantly, it really was their judgment day as there was no escape.

In my parent's young days some of the corn was made into porridge oats for the family - but notoriously the milling equipment used to fail to separate the hard hulls from the edible crushed grain. Mum used to quote a neighbour who famously remarked that his porridge meal was so laced with hulls that "for every one that was eating it would take three to spit!!" Breakfast was not a pure pleasure in those days. When I was young the corn was all used as animal feed - crushed for cattle or pigs, or simply fed as whole grain to the hens to encourage them to lay more eggs. As with every crop, seed was saved for the following season.

Hay was a crop we had to handle one way or another for most of the year. The meadows grew ungrazed by livestock in the early Summer and the cutting of hay usually started in June when the meadow grass was long enough. A bachelor farmer was once asked when he was getting married and the answer was "I don't know, for everything I do depends on the weather." I heard it many years ago as a joke but it expresses perfectly the hard reality with which every farmer had to live in the community of my childhood. When the hay was cut, if you got three or four dry, breezy days, you had hay of the very best quality - green and powder dry. If there was rain the cut grass could simply rot, spoil and be lost - or the quality of the hay could be so poor that only starving cattle would eat it. In Donegal it was rare that hay could be saved easily or straightforwardly. It had to be shaken and turned and made into small 'laps' called 'grasscocks,' then formed into 'handshakins' and lastly build into rucks or 'cocks.' Of course it was only in the worst of weather conditions that all these stages were necessary, but whatever had to be done was done with rakes and pitchforks and direct manual labour. On every smallholding farm, as soon as a boy or girl was capable of handling the haymaking tools, they were haymakers - and so too were those on holidays from the city for the summer break, they were expected to form a migrant labour force! I had the impression that my cousins from Belfast regraded it as a novelty and fun, but we had to live with it all Summer. When the weather was good it could be very pleasant and the banter among relatives and neighbours working together would be mighty but when the meadow grass had moulded in sogging dampness, the smell of it used to make me feel sick. Such was the culture of that time that I never complained to Dad, Mum or Uncle Tommy that I was nauseated - better to endure than to be regarded as a lazy whining wimp! It all sounds harsh and even cruel now but it was the common atmosphere of everybody's life then. The last stage of all was the building of the huge 'haystack' in the farmyard. For this big day, help assembled from surrounding farms. In a former generation a céilí dance used to be held in the farmhouse to celebrate the climax of the haymaking season. In my early years, horse-drawn 'ruck-lifters' had come into use. It had a long rope and ratchet to pull the hay cock up onto the flat bed of a cart to be drawn by the horse to the farmyard. Previous to that the hay had to be forked loose onto an ordinary horse cart in the meadow for transport home. As with so many processes, the tractor with a hydraulic buck-rake on the back seemed to be a flying machine! There were special long- shafted pitchforks to lift the hay onto the long stack when it got high and it was shaped and looked like a thatched cottage when finished. It was thatched with rushes, cut and ready in advance to make it waterproof for the rough Winter ahead. Those hay stacks were works of art, built with inherited skill by tough, weather-beaten men, and I never knew of one damaged by storm. Grass ropes were made from the hay itself, by using a wire 'twister' and edging backwards from a man 'letting-out' the hay from a small pile. These homespun grass ropes were used both to tie down the hay cocks in the meadow and to secure the hay stack at the Harvest. It was usually a boy or girl who operated the twister and a man who let out the hay at the correct speed and quantity to make a good strong rope. This all meant that there was an adequate supply of hay for the cattle during the Winter. Of course it had to be handled loose and carried tied up in rope-bound bundles to the cows in the byre and to the store cattle out in the fields, on a twice- daily basis.

The only year when this age-old system of basic animal feed failed was 1961/62. It was a Saturday morning in September 1961 - the end of the hay-making season

- and as we started what we thought would be a normal day, Dad became concerned that the wind seemed to be getting strong. So he took my bother Ade with him down to the 'long meadow' in the valley to make some extra grass rope with which to tie down cocks of hay still at that stage out in the open fields. Meanwhile my first morning chore was to dig enough potatoes for the family during the weekend from the ridges of maturing spuds on the hillside down from the byre. I thought I had become weak and dizzy as every time I put my foot on the spade to effect another dig, I fell down. After a while I realised that the wind speed was so fast that it was blowing me off my feet. I could see Dad and Ade struggling to twist new rope in the meadow below. It was to be no ordinary day for this was Hurricane Debbie and I can still remember

Granda Tom McElhinney.

clearly most of the details about it. Cocks of hay on Copany hill across the valley, belonging to Uncle Tommy, rolled like giant easter eggs across the side of the hill. Mum was utterly frightened that a couple of big trees too close for comfort, would fall on the house - the main concern being Granny's limited physical capacity to get to any alternative place of safety. The trees were twisting in a way that had to be seen to be believed, but thankfully they remained erect. Mum made sure that they were cut for firewood before many months had passed! At one point it looked as though the byre roof would break up as the corrugated iron-sheet roofing was shaking fiercely. The cows were tied in their usual places and Dad decided that they would be safer out in the grazing fields so he and I ran in and released the cows as quickly as we could. Amazingly, despite being on top of the hill, all our buildings survived intact. Another vivid incident that fateful day occurred when Dad, Uncle Tommy, Ade and I were walking from one effort to save hay in the meadows, to another along a farm lane slightly elevated from the surrounding fields and with no hedges. Ade was then thirteen years old and very slight of build and weight. A shocking gust of wind literally lifted him off the ground. His foot hit Tommy hard on the shoulder and Tommy instinctively grabbed him by the foot and pulled him back to earth! Until that day I never thought or believed the elements could be so fierce or that the wind could roar so loudly. It was to be in the Caribbean that I would hear that roar again.

An amazing feature of Hurricane Debbie was that there was no rain, unusually it was a totally dry storm. If there had been the normal heavy fall of rain either during or after the wind it would have been impossible to salvage any of the scattered hay, and the consequences for livestock would have been catastrophic. Fortunately the dry conditions meant that the next day, the Sunday, could be used as an opportunity to rake up and gather the remnants of hay that had been blown into the hedges. Incidentally a few farmers had taken their hay home to the farmyard much earlier than usual and all such hay escaped the destruction with only minor damage to the thatch.

Irish Protestants until then didn't work on Sundays but such was the extremity that an exception was made. I worked with Dad and Ade worked with Tommy on that extraordinary Sunday but we ended up with at best a quarter of the hay we had before the storm of a century for our part of the world. A grim and scarce Winter followed and such was the limited economy that the farmers could not afford to buy alternative feed. I had never seen our cattle as thin as they were in the Spring of 1962 but the poor cows managed to calve and life went on.

The aforementioned crops; potatoes, oats and hay kept every farming family busy - but there was another important matter which gave rise to considerable manual labour as well - keeping the home fire burning! The most common solid fuel in Donegal was 'turf', dried peat from the bogs, which burned very mildly and gave out good heat for cooking and comfort. I remember as a very young child seeing Dad cutting turf on our own farm - the very last of an old bog bank in the deep organic ground of the valley. The downside was that after it was cut and worked in this way, it left behind a low, wet and almost totally infertile soil. Unfortunately we had a few acres of this sort of spoilt and useless ground. By the time I was old enough to work in the bog, we were using a mountain bog bank given to us by a good neighbour Tony, to whom it had been allocated by the Land Commission. Due to some bureaucratic mix-up our farm had never been granted such a plot but Tony worked on our farm and we on his, and Dad did some tractor work for Tony and part of this informal co-operation was that Tony allowed us the use of part of his mountain bog bank.

It was about three miles away, part of the mountain range that runs between the counties of Donegal and Tyrone.

The first stage was the cutting of the turf in the Spring or early Summer. The thick

As a baby, with mum

As a very young boy behind the plough!

Charlotte with Mary McMenamin
at Mary's first Communion

Granny at garden gate

heathery surface had to be pared off and set aside, thus creating a long strip about a yard wide across the edge of the bank. The depth of organic peat could be up to six feet, brown near the top and black deeper down. Then the turf were cut in square formations around a foot long, with a 'turf spade' designed for the purpose and thrown up onto the bank. This was hard work and I never mastered the skill of lifting the long, floppy and wet pieces of fresh peat up on the turf spade to where they were supposed to go, but Dad was good at it. My job at this stage was to load the soggy, slimy and heavy sods onto a wheelbarrow and wheel them across the rough grass and heather for scattering out to begin the drying process. Next they had to be turned and then after another week or two we 'footed' the turf - that is we propped about six of them up against one another to dry to another stage. When they were drier still, they were 'clamped' into a bigger pile to prepare them to be drawn out of the bank to the bog road for transport home. I once helped Uncle Tommy to bring turf home to the Crossroads by horse and cart. As the grey horse, Joey clapped along down from the mountain to the lower, greener hills where we lived, we both sat up high on top of the turf load and Tommy sang an old Irish song to the rhythm of the horse's steps; "O to be in Dun-na-Ree with a sweetheart I once knew." Life was lived then at a slow and steady pace, moving with the seasons. We handled those turf at every stage without labour-saving devices, we took it all for granted and each day as it came.

As with the hay, so too with the turf - everything depended on the weather. In a wet Summer, the turf could fail to dry or the boggy ground could get so wet that it would be impossible to get the turf all off the bank to the bog road for carting home. I remember one bad season when Dad, Ade and I had to carry the dry turf on our backs for hundreds of yards to the bog road. The ground was so wet that we only managed to retrieve the turf in November.

If the turf were not all got safely home to the turf shed at the gable-end of the house, the alternative fuel was firewood cut from the hedges and ditches of our own land. Indeed most of the time the hearth of any farmhouse was supplied with a combination of these two solid fuels. The preparation of firewood was another manual task involving a big crosscut saw operated by two men, to fell a tree and cut the thicker trunks and branches, a bow saw for the thinner branches and hatchets to split the cut logs. Because we had a stove, the wood had to be reduced so as to fit the firebox - thus increasing the work. I think of a Winter when Ade and I were in our teens, students at 'the Tech', with homework to do, working with Dad in the turf shed cutting firework until 10pm almost every evening. The previous Summer had been unfavourable and the turf were scarce and it was the only way to keep the vital fire going at no monetary cost - the expenditure was of brawn and sweat!

We had our own milk, eggs and fowl and the main component of our diet was our own home- grown potatoes - with seasonal vegetables added. These factors saved us from the worst consequences of poverty. Mum had forty or fifty hens and also ducks and geese and even a couple of guinea-fowl as a novelty. Turkeys were very important as they were sold for the Christmas market, bringing in a little money for our family's Festive Season.

One of my duties used to be to carry, in a 'jute' bag from farm to farm, roosters and drakes for breeding and also 'clocking hens' in the right mood for brooding on eggs to make them hatch out. They would dutifully sit on the eggs of any species even for much longer than it took their own eggs to hatch. A hen would brood on goose eggs, three times the size of her own and for four instead of three weeks and then wonder why her oversized 'chicks' took every chance to run into water! The farmers' wives knew how to work all these tricks, a turkey-hen could be coaxed along to lay a second clutch of eggs if her first clutch was brooded by a hen. Another chore I was given was to take our turkey-hen at the right moment in her cycle of fertility, to meet her boyfriend - sort of indirect sex education! Farm youngsters would often be sent to carry fertile eggs to be set under a clocking hen. On one famous occasion Ade and I fetched goose eggs from Granny Maggie at the Crossroads and we fell out over some vital matter as we came along the 'cart road' in the valley towards the house. I chased Ade and hit him with the small bag containing the precious eggs and Mum came running down the hill to rebuke me severely and immediately requisitioned the eggs. The reckoning was that eggs so abused could never hatch but as a clocking hen was ready to do her part, they were set anyway. The brooding period was thirty days and after two weeks the eggs of any waterfowl could be tested for fertility by floating them in lukewarm water. The day of decisive proof arrived and the eggs were gently floated by Granny Jennie in that basin of tepid water just so. Lo and behold a slight kick from within shook each egg and the water trembled. My skin was spared, the goslings came out and became geese, and all was well that ended well.

In the keeping of fowl on small family farms in those days, there were a few public enemies every farmer wanted to kill, and Dad and other farmers would

My father

My mother

The Bustards, my mother's family

With great aunt Manie and Ade

band together to do just that when there were attacks on somebody's flock. Top of the wanted list came the fox - and he was joined in the 1960's by the mink after they started to escape from the cages in which they were farmed for fur production. Magpies would destroy eggs if they could get at them in the hen's nests. The hawk would prey on young chicks in the farmyard. All of the above were hunted down and destroyed at any and every opportunity and a ransom was paid to anyone who could produce the dead body of any of these enemies. This ransom was administered by a Publican in Main Street, Donegal, Tommy Galinagh. As I cycled to town for Mum's messages one week, I had six dead magpies in an old bag attached to my handlebars. I stopped at Tommy's pub, propped my bike at the kerbside and went in to see the boss - a small very friendly man. When we came out again, a big dog was disappearing round the corner, twenty yards away, with my old bag-full of dead magpies firmly clasped in his mouth! Tommy simply asked me how many corpses were in the bag, opened his till and handed me the few shillings with a confident wink. It was really only small change, but it seemed like a great fortune to me at the time.

A dog, such as our small white terrier, Spring, who could bring out a fox by the throat from a hole or culvert pipe, was highly prized indeed. Dad would be ready with his single barrel shotgun loaded to finish the fox off instantly - sometimes leaving a hole you could see through into the middle of the fox's body.

Our farmhouse and other buildings were on the hilltop, and for all my years at home, water supply was a problem. There were two categories of water, clean and 'rough.' Clean water was fit for human consumption, drinking, making tea etc., and it had to be carried in clean buckets from a clean well - ideally a spring well. Such a well was always in low ground and that meant for us that it had to be carried up the hill. Rough water was for the livestock to drink, for washing clothes, potatoes before cooking, or for washing the human body. Rough water could be caught from the roof or taken from a clay well, sunk in a field drain by the roadside. When we got a very dry Summer, even the rough water supply, no problem in the Winter, became a serious crisis. I remember returning after a long day's work in the bog and Mum had to send Ade and myself with the tractor two miles away to fill two big old creamery cans with water from an almost dry river- bed. After driving up the river to a pool, we came home with about twenty gallons of desperately needed water for washing etc. The great thing about a true spring well was that it never ran dry no matter how long the drought lasted.

Our precarious limited income was a fact only vaguely known by me during my childhood and youth and I know now that my parents and grandmother did everything to protect us from the worry of it. All my life I have felt that I could at least to some extent, understand poverty. One day whilst in Dublin for Committees, I was walking in O'Connell Street with my friend Rev. Ken Todd. As we passed Clearys Department Store, I told Ken how I always thought of my Mum when there as she knitted garments for Clearys throughout my childhood years. I remember how complicated some of the patterns used to be - with as may as four colours of wool being worked at one time. When next I was in Ardnagesson with Mum, I told her about my conversation with Ken, and then I said "You must have found the money from that work for Clearys very useful." Somewhat to my surprise she said, "I never got a penny out of it." When I asked why, she said to me; "Where did you think Santa got those presents left for you on Christmas mornings over those years?" Clearys had a catalogue and the craft worker could build up credit during the year and order for Christmas. The postman delivered when we were safely in school, and we were never without a pleasant surprise on the Festive Day. The penny dropped on this for me only a year or so before Mum died when I was in my sixties. As you live you learn and some of us are very slow learners.

My first day at school is etched on my memory as clearly as any other. I remember leaving with Mum on her bicycle. I sat on the home-made extra seat fitted behind her own saddle at the back of the bike - a seat that Dad had made - leaving Mum with a bicycle built for two. I can still see Dad and Ade waving us off as we passed the farmyard. Drumnahoul School was built in the nineteenth century among the green fields and I had never seen it before that day. When we got inside and Mum handed me over to Miss Armstrong, I refused to sit in the strange furniture everyone else was sitting in. Each long desk had a seat of the same length attached to it by bolted heavy iron fittings. They were the common school furniture of 1952, but you would have to visit a museum to see anything like them today. I cried bitterly as I simply didn't know what to expect. The genuine ignorance of children, and especially in the country parts, before the modern media came along, can scarcely be imagined now. I was six years old and the truth is that my education got off to a very slow start. Matters were not helped by the fast turnover of Teachers as they often stayed for only one or two years. It was only when Miss Alicia Kee (later Mrs. Duncan) came, that my education got off the ground. The main factor was that I liked her and she was able to communicate effectively and bring my learning up to speed. All my life I have been grateful to Miss Kee. There were only around fifteen pupils in Drumnahoul during my nine years there and the Primary School leaving age in the Republic of Ireland then was fourteen. With my birthday in early July, I remained at Drumnahoul until I was effectively fifteen and the Teacher for my last year was Miss Ella Morrow. By this time she was also my Sunday School Teacher and had a telling spiritual influence on me.

During that final year at our local school, a past pupil of the school, Rev. William Graham called in to see his successors in the old desks. He pointed at me and asked me what I planned to do with my life. Somewhat to my own surprise, I said I wanted to be a Minister. Mr. Graham, a dignified Anglican of the 'old school' said that he felt sure that would indeed happen.

At such a small school, the one Teacher had to impart the curriculum of eight grades and for the majority of the pupils their education finished with what was called 'The Primary Certificate.' Dad was keen that Ade should benefit from a technical education so in 1961 he went to Donegal Vocational School to see the Headmaster, Mr. Paddy Rooney. After they had discussed Ade's case, Mr. Rooney said, "Did you say you have another son?", so the conversation moved to me. The result was that Dad came home to announce that there were places for both of us at 'The Tech.' in September. So Ade and I, two years apart in age, started the course together for two years and found Mr. Rooney, Mr. Plunkett and Miss Hegarty great Teachers. I was seventeen when I left the Tech., and all I wanted to do at that stage was farming. I had dreams of expanding my stock of sheep and an ambition to build up a herd of pigs. So Dad and I set about building a sizeable pig-house - at first intended for me - but he was the one to make use of it as things turned out.

My Sunday School attendance was largely determined by where we lived. Being as far as we were from our own Methodist Church in the town, it did not work out for Ade and me to attend Sunday School there as young children, but there was a good Church of Ireland Sunday School in Copany Barn less than a mile from our home. The Rector of Laghey conducted Evening Prayer there one Sunday per month and the Sunday School was held every Sunday. Ade and I joined Hannah Kerrigan's class in a barn loft over a cattle house, sitting on long wooden form seats without back rests. As there was no heating, we kept our overcoats on. Conditions were basic but Hannah was a great Teacher and the profound meaning of that Anglican doctrine in the Prayer Book sank into my mind in those years - as did the good pastoral example of Canon Jack Warner. When we were a little older, we also started to go to Sunday School at Donegal Methodist Church - run by Ella Morrow so effectively and with such utter sincerity and dedication. Many a Saturday night I sat in the kitchen washing my feet in a basin of water - whilst Granny Jennie examined me on both the Church of Ireland and Methodist Catechisms! Such foundations were to be of such importance for my future.

A great bonus of belonging to two Sunday Schools was that we got to attend two Christmas parties and we were the envy of many for that double privilege. One party was in Laghey for the children of that Parish and the other in Donegal for all the Protestant children. Two stuffings of cake, two Santas and two presents! The Donegal Santa always made a dramatic entrance as we all sang "Jingle Bells", a suitable chubby figure right out of an old Yuletide picture book, and we cheered our wee heads off every year! Andy Morrow (Santa) was one of the truly striking characters of my years at home in Donegal.

Another huge influence for good was the Boy's Brigade with Bertie Scott as Captain of 1st. Donegal and Roy Jackson, Bill Scott and Jackie Irwin as Officers. It could not be claimed that I cut a great dash in 1st. Donegal - although I did carry off the Religious Knowledge prize a few times. That may have been a sign of things to come, but I drifted out of the Company in my late teens without distinction. It was only in later years that I realised the vital imprint of the B.B. on my life.

In January 1965 the Faith Mission came to our locality. In those days they could be sure that their portable wooden hall would be filled with a congregation every night. They preached a simple fundamental message and sang old Gospel hymns about blood and fire, sin and salvation. It affected me in such a way as to make me acutely aware that my spiritual life needed urgent attention. I was not an unbeliever in God, or a cynical rebel against the Christian Faith, but a new and serious commitment was needed in order for me to genuinely answer the Gospel call in my life. I went to the ordinary Sunday morning Service in Donegal Methodist Church, where I was a member and at the end of the Rev. Graham Hamilton's sermon I entered the Kingdom of God. It can be difficult to explain to those who have not travelled this evangelical road, but there was an actual moment as the Preacher closed the Pulpit Bible, when it happened. I knew in that instant, in a new way that I had never known before, that Jesus Christ is risen and alive for ever and his love and saving grace folded my whole being in a fresh and real experience. As I rode my bicycle the four miles home, I sensed and knew that I was living in a different world. It was observed of St. Francis of Assisi that he was so different after his conversion that it was as though he were standing on his head - and I can identify with that radical transformation in the whole perspective of life. In my case it refocused and renewed a sense of vocation to the ordained ministry that had been with me all my life.

I forgot about the pigs, sold the sheep and went to work in Magees Tweed Factory in Donegal Town for a year. It proved to be a good and positive time, a different working context from the farm with my Dad and a few others. It was my only period spent working in a structured industry and in the fullness of time it would help me to understand those whose workplace is a factory. It also left me free to make a move away from home, should some door of opportunity open for me. It is much more straightforward and clean-cut to resign from an industrial job than to have to sell livestock at short notice.

The hilltop farmhouse and the surrounding hills, Donegal Town and the nearby villages, the wonderful view of hazy Ben Bulbin, Co. Sligo to the South, Barnes Mōr to the North, Lough Eske and the majestic Bluestack Mountains in many a glorious sunset to the West, this was the tranquil setting of my life for twenty years. Often I would go out to Town Lough to inspect the livestock after a long day labouring at the hay or the turf, as darkness slowly began to descend. I could stand above Lough Rea, with its ring of pure white water lilies, and listen to cattle and donkeys roaring, sheep bleating and dogs barking for miles around. Basic faith in the God of Creation was simply natural.

Granny Jennie was a keen gardener and in my early years had a well-planned flower garden at the front of the house. After her husband, Bob bought the adjoining farm in the valley, he made a 'cart-road' from the house to the Lower Road. Granny was young and fit then and she planted clumps of daffodils all the way alongside the cart road from the house to the public road. It was always a beautiful sight in the Springtime when those blooming yellow flowers were dancing in the breeze in winding rows down the hillside and across the valley, for half a mile.

THE TALE END OF DONEGAL

Donegal Church

During the Advent Season, the 'Mummers' were a common feature of our rural culture. It was a strong inherited tradition among boys, and some girls, when I was young. We disguised ourselves with rags, old clothes and straw, formed a troop to visit farmsteads and rehearse an old set drama - always in a mumbled voice to avoid recognition! Among the characters portrayed were Oliver Cromwell, Big Head and Little Wit and Wee Doctor Brown - each with their own mummers rhyme. In reality it was an obscure excuse for begging - even though we had to sing at least a few verses of a song before a few pence were dropped into the rattling box.

Many a dark night I spent at it, with two or three friends - over hedges and ditches and through cart roads and fields. It could be hard going but the reward that always lay ahead was that you could swagger through the town on Christmas Eve with money in your pocket!

CLIFF COLLEGE

My initial theological education, building on a solid foundation of Sunday School instruction, was in a Local Preachers' Class led by the Revs Graeme Hamilton, Jim Williamson and later Aubrey West and my fellow students were Jack Moore and Arthur Morrow. There I learnt a great deal about the Bible, Theology and Worship and my awareness of a call to the ministry grew with that growing knowledge.

Mum once told me that before I was born she dreamt that I would be a Minister and there were family stories from my early years that seemed to point in that direction, but everybody knows that such things can often be nothing more than wishful thinking. More significantly a feeling of destiny developed in my mind during this period as I reflected on and prayed about my future.

Cliff College Derbyshire

In the Summer of 1966, when I was twenty, I fell deeply in love with Phyllis Harron whom I had known from childhood and whose grandmother was Becky Wray, our next-door-neighbour. Phyllis lived in faraway Belfast and somehow the relationship drew my heart away from the hills where I once thought I would spend my life.

With a fellow student

I had heard about Cliff College and the vague idea had entered my head that it might be the right place for me, so one Sunday after service I asked Rev. West to enquire into the possibility of my going there. A few days later I got a phone call at work from Mr. West asking me to call at the Manse on my way home as a brochure about Cliff had arrived with him. When I remarked that the response was swift to his request, he told me that he hadn't yet written the letter and that the College must have sent out some general publicity to Ministers!

That was early March 1967 and in one month I was in Cliff College. More detail would be boring now, but I felt that 'God had set before me an open door.' Exalted thinking about destiny and vocation is all very well but to do the necessary academic work to qualify is what keeps your two feet on the ground. The idea of answering God's call and doing His Will was very much in my mind, but so too was the salutary reality that I had none of the academic certificates required to offer as a candidate for the Ministry. I knew that this was the opportunity I had been longing for, to improve my educational standing.

It was because students came to Cliff from so many parts of the world and could arrive at any time of the year, that the College until that time retained the policy of taking in new students at the beginning of any term. A few other new people started with me but we were going into a student body well established from the previous September. The majority of our classmates were full of their experiences on the pre-Easter Missions - of which we knew nothing. I found myself listening to accents I had only previously heard on B.B.C. Radio programmes. When the Lectures started I was grateful for our small Local Preachers' Class in the lower hall in Donegal Town Methodist Church, and I found to my delight that I could follow the College Course quite well.

Overall, that first whirlwind Summer Term was something of a culture shock to me. It was my first time living permanently away from home, with my own laundry to wash, and living in an institutional community of eighty students, so different from the home farm. But Cliff was also in the country - the Peak District of Derbyshire - with its hills and mountains, green fields and farms.

The College Principal and Old Testament Tutor was the Rev. Howard Belben, a Cambridge graduate and quintessential English gentleman. I remember initially being struck by his upper class politeness and polished culture, but the more I got to know him, the more I realised what a true saint and scholar he really was. I could always approach him and he helped, advised and wisely led me through my time at Cliff.

The Rev. Malcolm Whyte taught Theology very effectively and was my Teacher for 'British Constitution' as an academic subject. He was full of all kinds of wit, was hopeful of a Labour seat in the Commons (for Plymouth) but Dr. David Owen beat him to that. He became an outstanding Comprehensive School Headmaster and late in his career, Superintendent of Central Hall, Westminster.

The Rev. Royston Emms, with his lilting Welsh accent, taught New Testament and gave me my first lessons in Greek. He was first trained as a Teacher and later returned to the educational field.

Mr. Frank Blackwell taught Pastoral Studies and Evangelism. His background was in Black Country industrial management and he had a wealth of knowledge and experience to impart.

Part of the traditional working of Cliff was that every student took part in three sessions, lasting two hours each, of manual work on the college and grounds - six hours per week. Because I came from a farm, I was sent to work on the garden at Holly Tree, the home of Miss Doris Hallam.

Miss Hallam was a Primary School Teacher who did some work at the College, teaching remedial English to those who needed extra help with their language. The only payment she wanted was that a suitable student should keep her garden in order. So I went up Cliff Lane to the old stone house called 'Holly Tree' with its sizeable garden, to do what I could to keep the Summer growth down and tidy things up generally.

When the Half Term Break came, she invited me to stay at Holly Tree, and when Phyllis came over she stayed there too and before we knew it we were part of 'the Holly Tree Family' headed by 'Aunty Dot.' There were around thirty families who were part of it - all former Cliff students and their families located in different parts of the world. We came and went visiting Holly Tree and Aunty Dot and for twenty years it was our home in the North of England. We had a great relationship with this wise Christian lady, single and childless, but a spiritual mother to so many. She was also an excellent Preacher and many a congregation of mine, in the Caribbean and in Ireland, was held spellbound by her when she was lodging with us at the Manse.

The old Cliff College Summer Treks, with the students pushing a barrow cart on the road and camping along the way, had been developed into Summer Holiday Missions at various seaside locations around Britain and I was assigned to a small team going to the Isle of Man. We preached and carried out children's activities on the beaches at Port Erin and Port St. Mary in the South of the island and slept in vestries and church halls. I felt nervous preaching to packed congregations on the Sundays - B.B. and G.B. Companies on camping exercises all out in force to fill the pews. Until then I had never faced such crowds to preach. It was all new and exciting, part of the challenge I was having to rise to at that time and I enjoyed every minute of it. My twenty-first birthday was spent on that Mission and the local Methodist people organised a lovely party for me in the church hall in Port Erin - cake, cards, presents and even a request on a local radio programme! One of those truly pleasant and most memorable surprises.

By the end of that first term I had become used to the atmosphere of Cliff and I revelled in the life of the place. I was travelling to preach all over the North Midlands as appointed by the College or with groups of friends from among the students as a sort of private and extra arrangement from time to time. Sunday evenings in the College dining room were always interesting times, as we related our experiences of the day - the journeys and churches and the characters we met. I returned home to Donegal in August for a brief Summer Break - and my friends in the Donegal, Ballintra and Inver Circuit organised a Social Evening at which I was presented with a very generous gift of enough money to cover all my travel costs, plus purchase of books etc., needed for my time at Cliff. My gratitude to those who organised it and contributed to it, has never faded.

All along I knew that a big test would come for me in the Autumn Term. In

(L to R) Robert Russell, Johnny Morris & myself - the three Irish students at the time

September I had to get to work on my G.C.E. 'O' Levels in addition to the College Course, which was designed as a full-time programme of study in its own right. It meant that I had to attend extra classes in the evenings after the normal day of lectures and that I had to try to keep abreast of a large number of subjects. I needed five 'O' Levels for entry to the Irish Methodist Ministry so I started to prepare for six subjects, thus allowing for one failure. My aim was to be in a position to apply for the Ministry as soon as possible after leaving Cliff. I got up at 5.30am on two mornings per week in order to put in enough private study time, and with coffee to keep myself awake and alert!

At the end of that Term and as Christmas 1967 approached, the notable news was that Foot & Mouth disease had hit the farms of England in a devastating way. At night we could see the sky lit up with the burning of slaughtered cattle and other livestock. Fear gripped the rural communities of the British Isles. I travelled to Liverpool, not knowing whether or not the Belfast ferry would be sailing. The Belfast boat was going, but the Government of the Republic of Ireland had forbidden the Dublin boat to sail until further notice. In the face of all the dire warnings about the matter, I made the painful decision not to go to Donegal for Christmas. I just could not bear the thought that I might be responsible for bringing Foot & Mouth home with me, knowing that the consequences would be the slaughter of all our family's livestock and many neighbours as well. Phyllis' parents very kindly put me up for the fortnight at Ava Drive in South Belfast.

Ivan and Phyllis at Cliff

I preach in the open air, Port St. Mary, Isle of Man

Phyllis with Aunty Dot at Holly Tree

In the New Year of 1968 I sailed the Irish Sea again, and back by a now familiar route of public transport to North Derbyshire for the Spring Term. My heavy burden of study continued and I had minimal time for any kind of social life. With Phyllis far away that was not a problem, we simply wrote to each other once a week and I wrote home to Ardnagessson weekly too. Nevertheless I didn't become a recluse but very much enjoyed lots of friendships with my fellow students. Robert Russell and David Jarman were among those I formed life-long contact with although, in the nature of the case many acquaintances faded when we all left the College. A great comfort was that I had my local home at Holly Tree, just up the lane, and I could literally go there at any time.

During Lent, as plans were being made for the annual pre-Easter Missions, I was astonished to find myself appointed to lead the smallest of three Teams going out on this exercise. The two much larger Teams were led by College Tutors and I felt daunted by the duty and responsibility being given to me but I knew I had to rise to it and that I could learn much from it. Six of us went to the mining community of Ollerton in Nottinghamshire part of the Mansfield Circuit, to work with the Rev. Harry Dennis, formerly a missionary in Africa. There we joined with theological students from the Anglican and Baptist traditions to form an ecumenical Team on an outreach mission to the whole town of Ollerton. We had a great week, with students from Oxford and Cliff College joining together to visit door-to-door and make our witness for Christ in the pubs, clubs and churches of that industrial township. When I preached at a Final Rally, I felt deeply moved to see people coming forward at the end to make new responses to the Christian Message.

It was on that high spiritual note that I went on to Liverpool and overnight by ferry to Belfast. Whilst I wasn't among the starving poor in those student years, I wasn't rich either and one way of saving money was not to book a cabin on the Irish Sea ferry. The seats in the lounge were in fixed rows back-to-back, leaving a convenient space between the backs of the seats where I could crawl in, put my head on a life-jacket and sleep.

On this journey, when I lay down I heard a sharp sound as of some objects falling on a hard surface, but thought nothing of it. When I woke up and crept out in the morning, a man was sitting in one of the seats watching for me. He drew my attention to a small pile of coins on the floor, and said, "There you are, that's your money - if fell from your pockets after you lay down last night." A refreshing spirit of honesty to do ones heart good. Many were the long conversations I had with my fellow passengers, often labouring Irishmen who had worked all their adult lives in England.

My 21st birthday party in Port Erin, Isle of Man

Unlike the Christmas holidays, there was no Foot-&-Mouth danger at Easter and I was free to go on to Donegal. How I enjoyed just roaming the fields, visiting relatives and neighbours and chatting with my own family in the farmhouse kitchen.

My most important appointment on that visit to Ireland was at the Methodist Manse in Ballyclare. I had responded to an advert in the Irish Christian Advocate, then the newspaper of the Methodist Church in Ireland, for a Lay Evangelist in the Ballyclare Circuit. This really meant Lay Pastoral Assistant and I knew that such work experience would be ideal for me, were I to be accepted as a Candidate for the Ministry. I travelled by bus from Belfast to Ballyclare and was met at the Station by the Rev. Willie Twinem - easy to recognise in his deep clerical collar, dark grey overcoat and black hat. We walked the few hundred yards to the Manse where Mrs. Twinem soon served coffee and we discussed the work that awaited me. Mr Twinem impressed upon me what he clearly saw as the main priority, "Your job is to keep the Doagh people happy." As we walked back to the Bus Station, he explained that he expected me to take up the position as from 1st. July.

Back at Cliff College for my fourth and final Term, the intense academic pressure that had borne down upon me in both the Autumn and Spring Terms eased considerably. Having been there a whole year I had already completed the Course set by the College itself, and my Diploma would be duly issued in June. This all meant that I could now concentrate all my study time and effort on my GCE. 'O' Levels. Those subjects would normally be studied over several years in a secondary level school and I had just one academic year in which to prepare for the exams - and that on top of another full-time course. It was impossible to predict what the outcome would be, but one great advantage was that I had the Summer Term 1968 to devote entirely to these important studies, so vital for my future!

I passed on all six subjects, which meant that I could go ahead and offer myself as a candidate for the Ministry of the Methodist Church in Ireland.

The fifteen months I spent at Cliff College was in so many ways the most significant short period in my life. This remains true even today as I reflect on it all in retirement and there are two main reasons why it is so. First, I went to Cliff with none of the academic requirements for candidature for the Ministry and I came away with them all. Second, the basic foundational Biblical and theological course of Cliff stood me in good stead in the later training for the Ministry, and throughout my career in the Church.

There were additional benefits too - I gained social experience and confidence and met people from every region of the world. My fellowship with the West Indian students was very special and those friendships would lead to years spent in the Caribbean.

If I have Miss Kee to thank for setting my primary education on a sound footing, I have Cliff College to thank for doing the same for my adult education. It would have taken me many years of correspondence courses or evening classes after work to gain what I achieved at Cliff in such a short time. Cliff College transformed and enriched my life beyond description.

THE TALE END OF CLIFF COLLEGE

One of the great traditions of Cliff in the old days was the Whit Monday College Anniversary. It was a weekend of frenetic activity with large crowds of mainly Methodists from all over Britain in attendance for the sheer inspiration of it all. The students became the workforce to deliver the logistics, and we had to work to the point of exhaustion - but one had no problem sleeping in a tent out in the grounds whilst some nice, paying guest occupied ones student room! I was part of the catering staff - effectively a waiter on one of the long trestle tables in Cliff Hall, struggling to serve eleven hundred meals overall.

There would be three or four Services of Worship or rallies in progress simultaneously at different locations in the surrounding fields, with special speakers - mostly 'heavyweights' like Colin Morris and on one famous occasion Billy Graham - to stir up the spirits of the faithful. I was appointed to testify before the Terrace congregation, assembled at the front of the main building on the lawn and I was given a time to be in the Principal's Study to get ready.

It was quite a mental adjustment from Cliff Hall as chaotic as a refugee dining facility, to the sedate culture of a room lined with thousands of shelved books and full of famous evangelical leaders. The President of the British Methodist Conference, the Rev. Dr. Evanway Morgan was there - as was the Rev. Dr. John R.W. Stott, who was to preach on the Terrace. Dr. Stott felt mortified because he had come too informally dressed - no clerical collar and in a sports-jacket. The Principal beckoned me over and whispered to me: "Ivan please go and put on your Irish tweed jacket, it will reassure Brother Stott." I quickly obeyed and it would not be the only important moment in my life when I would wear something made by my former employers, Magee of Donegal.

BALLYCLARE

I got back to Ireland from Cliff at the end of June 1968 and had time for a short trip to Donegal before taking up my appointment as a Lay Evangelist or Pastoral Worker on the Ballyclare Circuit. One important thing I brought with me from Ardnagesson was my Dad's three-speed bicycle. It was old as Dad had it as long as I could remember and it had seen better days but it was working and it would take me round the roads of South East Antrim.

My Superintendent, the Rev. William S. Twinem had a reputation for severity towards his junior colleagues. At first that seemed to be confirmed when he lost no time in telling me how disappointed he was to hear that I had a girlfriend. As my

Ballyclare Methodist Church

age was then twenty-two I found that remark slightly odd but kept quiet for a few seconds. I then sensed that his concern was over the danger of distraction from my work and I assured him that I would meet my girlfriend on my one day off per week and that there would be no interference with my work in the Circuit. But it did leave me feeling that I must be discrete about any visits Phyllis might make to Ballyclare.

Soon, the Twinem family were off on their Summer holiday - a pastoral exchange with a Minister from the Isle of Man. I called at the Manse, out of courtesy, to see the temporary pastor and his wife - to find that he was a pipe-smoking liberal and very different from Mr. Twinem.

My assignment during the Superintendents holiday was to make my way through the Ballyclare visiting list which was fairly extensive and the preaching routine took me around all three churches; Ballyclare, Balynure and Doagh. I was effectively in pastoral charge of the small Methodist Church and community of Doagh. When the Rev. Twinem returned, he was delighted with the amount of visiting I had done and with the reports he had heard from the families about the visits and all was well for the rest of the year. I soon came to love and respect Mr. & Mrs. Twinem and their very committed Christian family. It would be difficult to think of another Manse family in which all the children devoted their professional working lives to the cause of Christ and the mission of the Church.

I always knew exactly where I stood with Willie Twinem and I learnt a great deal

through working with him for that year. I went to the Manse once a week for a working lunch; the meal was wholesome and the conversation serious and meaningful and we worked well together. On a few occasions I got a sincere and gentle rebuke from my experienced superior but I always knew I deserved it and needed to learn from my mistakes.

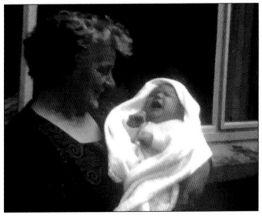

My landlady, Mrs. Tyrell with our son Mark

My Landlady was Mrs. Jean Tyrell, a childless widow who also had two Teachers from Ballyclare High School as boarders in the house. It was the only time I ever lived in digs, and like my experience of that year in general, it was a very positive and happy relationship which lasted as long as she lived.

Mr. Bill Montgomery, a prominent member of the Ballyclare Church taught Classics at Ballyclare High and he always undertook to teach some elementary Greek to the succession of young candidates for the Ministry working on the Circuit. Roy Emms at Cliff had already given me a start and Mr. Montgomery gave me a lesson each week to prepare for the exam in the Spring of 1969. His wife Frances, had my name in the pot for Tea with the family before I left each time - a truly lovely couple and family.

My candidature for the Ministry proceeded successfully in 1969 and by Conference in June I knew that I would be going to Edgehill. I went back home to Donegal for July, August and September to do three jobs: First I worked in Magee Menswear and Shoe Shop six days per week, full time. Second my dad gave me the use of a pen in the piggery to fatten a dozen pigs. Thirdly I preached every Sunday, morning and evening to the holidaymakers in Bundoran Methodist Church. I had no organist to help me and I had to recruit a musician from among the congregation for both Services each Sunday. The interesting thing about this was that I found a good organist in the first pew I approached almost every Sunday and I was never left without an organist at any Service. Some might say "just good luck," others, "God provides," I prefer the latter. I was grateful for the help of kind strangers, amidst the intense schedule of a very busy summer of such varied and committed work.

Phyllis and I took a week in the Isle of Man before my new college term started. The Rev. Juan Thompson and his wife Margaret generously accommodated us at the Manse in Port Erin. This was a contact that went back to the Cliff Mission there in 1967.

THE TALE END OF BALLYCLARE

I was around six weeks in Ballyclare when I encountered the Ulster phenomenon then known as Paisleyism and it really did give me a fright. I called at a house and after a few introductory pleasantries the man asked me what I thought of Captain O'Neill. This was the Anglo-Irish aristocratic gentleman who was then Prime Minister of Northern Ireland. He was a moderate Unionist with a vision and aspiration to integrate the two traditions, Unionist and Nationalist, Protestant and Catholic and to create an inclusive political system open to all.

My personal politics did not match Capt. O'Neill's at every point but I did very much admire his vision and courage. So, when I was asked what I thought of him I gave what I regarded as an inoffensive answer: "I think he's a good man."

I expected this to lead to the sort of common talk about public life in the Province that was daily fare. Instead it was the proverbial 'red rag to a bull.' The man suddenly flew into an uncontrolled rage, verbally insulted me and stamped out banging the door. His mild-mannered wife was left to normalise the atmosphere before I left in a state of shock. I was learning fast that I had come home to a country where politics had to be handled with the utmost care - as the subject was potentially explosive.

EDGEHILL

On the first Sunday in October 1969, Ade drove me to Belfast to start my standard training in the usual way in preparation for the Ministry. Mum came along too - her very first time in Belfast. Mr father's sister Margaret, single and living in her own small terraced house on the Donegall Road, provided me with an alternative base to College (like Holly Tree when I was at Cliff), during my student years in Belfast, so that was where Ade and Mum left me.

The next day I walked with my suitcase and briefcase to our Methodist Theological College in leafy Lennoxvale, Malone Road - the University part of town. I well remember feeling as I walked through the large iron gate, with the name 'Edgehill' wrought into its top bars, that I was walking into the Methodist Ministry. I was crossing the Rubicon and it was a good feeling but I also knew that I had three years of challenging study to face, including the learning of Greek and Hebrew!

The building was old, but it was comfortable enough to live and study in. There were six successful candidates that year, so we soon got to know one another quite well. The overall student number seldom reached twenty, due to the relatively small size of the Methodist denomination in Ireland.

The teaching staff of Edgehill consisted of two Ministers - the Principal was the Rev. Richard Greenwood, whose academic speciality was Ancient Oriental Languages, and the Tutor was the Rev. Dr. Richard (Dick) Kingston, a Philosopher. There was no Secretary and no administrative staff. The office of Matron had been discontinued just prior to my time, but there was a Cook and two Room Maids.

When the Cook moved on at one stage, Mrs. Greenwood had to undertake that heavy load of work at short notice. Oddly, the College had its own flock of laying hens kept inside on deep litter, to supply the kitchen with eggs, and for one of my years there I was the obvious choice of my fellow-students as 'Henman!' Life was not easy for the Principal and Tutor - a fact of life not much understood by us young students. We were nearly all single and with little appreciation of the management issues and difficulties faced by our leaders.

One section of the dormitories was occupied by 'lay' students, those studying in other faculties of Queens University; Medicine, Architecture, Economics etc. This was quite good for us budding Theologians, as it kept us all in touch with the wider, secular world.

There was a joint teaching arrangement with the Presbyterian Union College - where the Teachers all carried the title 'Professor.' The result was that we had an excellent Faculty, with a high quality of scholarship across the whole range of our subjects. I was particularly inspired by Prof. John M. Barclay in Church History and Prof. 'Jock' McFadden in Biblical Theology. Dick Kingston was my confidant and Pastor and our friendship lasted for life.

Front of College

College Entrance

Phyllis and I got engaged during this time; I would rise from my evening private study time to meet her coming off duty as a Nurse at the City Hospital. We would meet in Elmwood Avenue and have a snack at the Montmarte Café on Strandmillis Road and then I would walk her home over the Lagan Bridge to the Ormeau precincts where she lived and I walked back to Edgehill. Those were the days of pure romance!

Most of the Methodist students were not on the B.D. Degree course and I was one of that majority. It meant the doing of a three-year course, learning the original Biblical languages and being examined to a high standard in the full range of theological subjects and coming out at the end without a degree. But I have to say that it never troubled me in the least; all I wanted to do was to be in the pastoral ministry - higher academia never really appealed to me. I enjoyed the studies, I knew I needed such learning as I was gaining and College was a happy and positive phase of my life but I never was an academic scholar.

I thought that it was important for me to gain more experience of the life of the Church in all its diversity at this training stage and there was the opportunity to do so. The College year was so structured that as a student you had June, July August and September as a long Summer break and I decided to look for pastoral work in the two Summers available.

During the Summer of 1970 I worked in what was then called the Agnes Street Circuit, which meant the entire Shankill Road district of West Belfast from Peter's Hill to Lower Ballysillan. There were three Methodist Churches each with its own Minister. The Superintendent Rev. Fred Aiken was in Shankill Road

/ Berlin Street, the Rev. Harold Good was at Agnes Street and the Rev. Tom Magowan (newly returned from Jamaica) was at Woodvale.

My main job for the four months was to visit as many of the Methodist homes as I could following the family lists supplied by the Ministers. The first task was to make my own visiting list from the three I was given. Such a pastoral visiting list was usually hand-written in a small book that would fit into your jacket pocket in those untechnical days.

I put in around six hours of visiting per day, five days per week. After all, I had little else to do apart from preparing for a couple of Services each Sunday - filling in for the Ministers when they were on holidays. I lodged at Auntie Margaret's home and rode a little old fixed-wheel bicycle all over Shankill, going through the Lower Falls on the way to and from work. It was a valuable pastoral exercise in the inner city, a very different context from my own roots in the country, from which I gained a great deal in terms of preparation for my pastoral life. I was also able to do a little reading in advance of the studies I knew I would be doing when College resumed in the Autumn.

In the Summer of 1971 I was employed by the North Belfast Mission in York

Tutors and students - I am on the far left seated

Street, to help with the pastoral care of the one thousand plus families on the community list of that church, as well as with the social work of the Mission. It was a short period that stretched and developed my pastoral capacity considerably. One morning I went into the Mission Office to discover that my duty that morning was a Funeral - yes, all on my own - something I had never done before!

I also had to dispense grocery vouchers and used clothing to the poor and needy who came to the Mission every day for help. I had to pray hard and simply learn on the job as for much of the time the regular staff were away on holidays or engaged elsewhere in the multitude of duties to be done.

It was also during this summer of 1971 that I came face-to-face with the Northern Ireland Troubles, which by this stage had reached a new level of intensity.

As a child I had listened to my grandparents' generation telling horror stories about the old Irish Troubles in the First World War era and the 1920's. As I started to read some Irish history, I came to identify all of that with the War of Independence, symbolised by 1916 and the tragic Civil War which came later. I used to think that those dim and distant uncivilised times of long ago were over, never to return. It was a combination of the childhood notion that anything your grandparents talk about is ancient history, and a post-war youthful optimism that war would be no more. How utterly naive and wrong I was about all that!

When I returned from Cliff College to South Antrim in 1968, Ian Paisley was notoriously stirring the sectarian pot in Ulster. There were serious riots and security problems over the Apprentice Boys of Derry annual parade that year. Sadly, it was a sign of much worse strife to come. In the Summer of 1969, whilst I was treble-jobbing in Donegal, Belfast and the six Counties in general, exploded with riots and raw sectarian hatred. As Phyllis and I were on the Airport Bus going up the Grosvenor Road on our way to the Isle of Man, we could see the makeshift barricades of old furniture, fridges, cookers and waste timber at the end of each side street. There was a sort of doomsday feeling about some parts of Belfast, whilst other neighbourhoods looked normal. New sectarian dividing lines began to appear in the working- class inner city and in the housing estates and these boundaries were acquiring great importance in local perception. It was all a sad sign of the decades of conflict that were to follow.

Harold Good and many other clergy used to gather at 168 Agnes Street to try to calm things down in the evenings, sometimes for months whilst the disturbances lasted. As the Shankill area is a Protestant enclave surrounded by Catholic territory, local nerves seemed to be on edge and such was the situation then that fear stalked the streets.

A group of us students from Edgehill used to join the clergy at Agnes Street, partly out of curiosity and partly to help if we could. Along with Harold and a group of others, I went out on one of the informal patrols to reassure people and when we walked off Shankill Road into a residential street, we were faced by a hail of live rifle fire - the soldiers thought we were petrol bombers!! The screech of the bullets going over our heads was a sound I had only previously heard on the old films about the Second World War. A kind family in Harold's pastoral care hastily admitted us to their terraced home, where we sat all night listening to gunfire, shouting, the banging of hard objects off police and army vehicles and the explosion of petrol bombs.

We had to try to communicate with the soldiers in the street through the letter-box slot in the door as it was too dangerous to open the door or a window and at 6 am an armoured vehicle came to take us back to Agnes Street. My memory of that short journey is of two factors; firstly the van was full of prisoners with their hands held above their heads and the clergy were the only free people on board, and secondly, the crunch of broken glass, masonry and stones under the heavy-duty tyres of the vehicle - the debris of a whole night of rioting.

Crowds used to gather at the Agnes Street / Shankill junction or at Peters Hill at the lower end of Shankill Road - depending on the latest local rumour. The police would be on hand in crowd-control formation to prevent an open sectarian confrontation. The police and crowd would line up to each other, some missile would be thrown from the crowd and all hell could and often did, break loose very quickly. Shop windows would be broken and when an eerie calm eventually came, looting openly took place. Sometimes the crowd would listen to the clergy and take the advice to disperse quietly and go home. Sometimes politicians would come to try to settle things down, and I was the one to stand on a soap box one evening using a loud-hailer to introduce Mr. Bill Craig. Mr. Craig was a right-wing Unionist who had resigned from Brian Faulkner's Government and he did his best to appeal to the crowd. But vain was the hope that they would heed Mr. Craig and we all beat a dignified retreat before battle commenced with the police once again!

In the Summer of 1971, while I was with the North Belfast Mission, a remarkable movement of population occurred. The sectarian boundaries were coming under pressure and changing position in various parts of Belfast in the very fluid circumstances that then existed. Eventually those dividing lines would become fixed as high 'peace-line' walls but at this early stage there was a feeling that ones family was not safe if members of the 'other side' lived nearby and that it might be wise to get out while the going was good. Accordingly the electrically-powered flat-bed milk delivery vans were commandeered by gangs of likely Loyalist lads, to move Protestant families out of perceived danger, to reside more securely among their own kind.

The migration I came to know about so intimately was from the North Queen Street area, near the Mission Church, up the Shore Road to Mount Vernon, Shore Crescent and Rathcoole. The milk floats could be seen by the score up and down the Shore Road every evening for an entire week. On the way out they were loaded high with household furniture and people clinging onto every foothold, and on the way back, empty to effect another free removal job. The families were going into houses and flats abandoned by Catholic families gripped by the same fear. Within the space of a week or two hundreds of households moved in this way - the fleet of milk delivery vans was only the most obvious part of it. Many others made their own arrangements and moved less visibly. Of course, there was no reference to the Housing Executive or to the private landlords who owned the properties and many of those involved were in the pastoral care of the Mission. Chaos reigned and it was hard to know for a while where some of our parishioners lived.

One family we knew had all their belongings loaded onto a vehicle and the lady of the house was then seated in the front beside the driver. The volunteer removal men asked her if she wanted to have the house burned, so that the other side couldn't get it. She gave a half-nod and a can of petrol was lifted from the foot-well where she was sitting, the hallway was splashed and a match thrown in. Her last sight of her former home was of a flash of flames destroying the place and she fainted. But the bottom line of the story was that the fresh evening breeze through the side window of the van going up the Shore Road, revived her - to unpack in one of the high-rise flats of Mount Vernon.

The fragmentation of the Unionist political cause, the Civil Rights Movement and the closure of the Stormont Parliament were all features of my student years. Rumours abounded that the Civil Rights organisation had been infiltrated by extremist Republicans with violent intent, and that a new I.R.A. was on the rise. People of moderate opinion tended at first to think that such perceptions were only motivated by political propaganda but sadly the nightmare started to come true.

My ministry proper had not yet begun, but in terms of life in this world in all its raw reality, I was growing up fast. Little did I know that I would be preparing to retire before those dreadful Troubles would be over, or that such tragic events would develop in the decades ahead, with such loss of life and limb.

THE TALE END OF EDGEHILL

On a night of fierce rioting on the Shankill Road, two of my fellow-students were doing some first-aid work with rioters who had been brought injured into 168 Agnes Street. One man with a very bloodied head was sitting on a kitchen chair while they tried to clean him up a bit. One was washing round his ear and discovered to his horror that effectively the ear had been severed, apart from a little skin at the front. No wonder that Belfast acquired the reputation of one of the world's war-zones!

THE NORTH BELFAST MISSION

I t was in your final year at College that you encountered for the first time, the Stationing Committee of the Methodist Conference and mere theological students going into their first year of probation for ordination were inevitably at the bottom of the priority list. But my peculiar circumstances had created stability for me. Phyllis and I had been accepted by the Methodist Missionary Society as suitable candidates for work overseas and the Irish Conference had given permission for that to happen after I had served one year of my probation in Ireland. The idea here was that when I would return to the home work I would have some experience to build upon. This meant that I was available for only one year and it so happened that there was a Circuit in transition that needed a junior Minister for one year -the North Belfast Mission.

The Superintendent was the Rev. Charlie Bain, who wanted to have me with him on that station. Due to the re-development of inner-city North Belfast and the proposed

Phyllis and I on our wedding day

Rev. C.H. Bain

routes for new motorway feeder roads, the old N.B.M. building in York Street would be demolished, along with hundreds of houses and shops in the Docklands, so the Mission would have to re-locate. Charlie Bain was faced with an extremely complex business agenda and it was by no means clear at first where the new Mission site would be. Among the features of this whole situation was the issue of ministerial staff. Until then there had been two ministers based in York Street but it now seemed possible that after the re-location the second minister at the Mission might no longer be needed due to amalgamation with another church with its own minister. So to North Belfast we went for the one year - although the eventual move of the Mission to Rathcoole would take longer than a year, as such complicated mills usually grind more slowly than expected.

My time at Edgehill ended in May 1972 and Phyllis and I got married in Desertmartin Parish Church, Co. Londonderry on Monday 29th. May. We had time for our honeymoon in Scotland before I took up my station as from 1st. July. The reason for our wedding venue was that Phyllis's brother the Rev. Jim Harron was Rector of Desertmartin and the journeys of our guests from Donegal and Belfast were of roughly equal distance. Jim and his first wife Ellen did everything to accommodate and arrange our wedding and we and our families and friends had the sort of enjoyable day a wedding aught always to be. We originally met as children in Ardnagesson when Phyllis and her parents were on holidays at her mother Susan's old home - the farm next door - and the relationship that led to marriage began in the summer of 1966. I left from Charlie Bain's Manse in North Belfast, with my brother Ade as Best Man and the Rev. Des Bain as Groomsman and Phyllis's

Our first Manse, Strathmore Park North

Bridesmaids were my two sisters Charlotte and Irene and Alison Harron made a very willing Flower-girl.

It was to lodge briefly with Charlie and Evelyn Bain that we returned from honeymoon - until the second N.B.M. Manse was available. Our first married home was the Epworth Manse, 25 Strathmore Park North, Belfast, where we lived for only three months. But it was long enough for an amusing and at the time noteworthy incident to happen. We woke up one bright summer morning to find a burglar in our bedroom. As we were in an old high Victorian bed, when the young man became aware that we were stirring, he crawled in under the bed to wait it out until we fell asleep again! What he didn't know was that we could see him in the mirror on the wardrobe door! We quickly decided (with whispers) that I should stay in the room whilst Phyllis would say audibly she was going to the bathroom. She then crept downstairs and phoned for the Police who arrived very quickly and arrested the chap from under the bed! I was famous among colleagues and friends for years as 'the man with a burglar under his bed' but we were fortunate that it all ended so peacefully and we could dine out on it as a true, funny story.

In the Autumn we moved to the Rathcoole Manse - destined to become offices and shop-units for the Mission in its new format as the Newtownabbey Methodist Mission - but still at this stage used as a Manse.

The Troubles impinged upon life more and more and vigilante groups of self-appointed community protectors were quickly replacing the clergy and people of genuine goodwill, who had patrolled the streets in menacing times, a few years before. The vigilantes were stopping traffic and questioning drivers (eg. as to whether you lived in Rathcoole) and threatening those who refused to take part in protests and strikes. They gave us a great deal of trouble at our Youth Club in the Church Hall in Rathcoole. They wanted to search boys and girls for knives and the Youth Leaders and I refused to let them in. They gathered in quite large numbers in our church grounds, each with a long baton and wrist strap attached. It was obvious for a while that they were trying to intimidate us and one of the local stories was that they were wanting to close down youth organisations in order to help them recruit more young men into their own ranks.

We repeatedly had to call the police for protection from them and at one stage a rumour began to circulate that they were planning an attack on me. Charlie Bain summoned a few of their leaders to the Rathcoole Church Hall and opened proceedings by saying that unless he were given an absolute assurance that there was no threat or danger to his colleague, he would leave straight away and drive to the B.B.C., where a journalist was waiting to record an interview with him. The media were keenly interested just then in the turn the whole vigilante scene was taking, and they knew that Charlie could damage their image severely by saying that they were engaged in such bullyboy tactics. They backed down at once saying that it was another person they were after - someone whose conscience had forbidden him to co-operate with them in a 'Loyalist Strike' and I was declared to be safe. A byproduct of that meeting was that life returned to normal at the Youth Club.

It was by this stage becoming obvious that the Provisional I.R.A. existed and was active in the fast-developing conflict and what we were seeing in Rathcoole and many other places was the rise of its mirror-image, the 'Protestant backlash,' the Loyalist Paramilitaries. One Saturday in this period, Phyllis and I were in the City Centre and on our way home up the Shore Road, when we met rank upon rank of masked men in paramilitary uniforms - literally by the hundreds - marching to the City Centre in a show of strength.

As a young married couple, we would sometimes decide to make a short visit to Phyllis' parents on the Ormeau Road. It meant driving in the mid-evening through Belfast - North to South - and going through the entire central thoroughfares, we might meet one or two cars and see only one drunk man staggering home. Fear of bombs in cars, pubs and shops and other forms of unpredictable violence had gripped the population and the social life of the City Centre had died away, Belfast had become a ghost town.

On the more personal level we were very happy and Phyllis got a nursing job at Greenisland Hospital. My work in the Mission under the benign direction of Charlie Bain, was a sheer delight. Charlie was a quiet saint of God, calm and serene and walked as closely with his Lord as anyone I ever knew. I have always counted it as one of the great blessings and privileges of my life to have worked alongside Charlie Bain as a student and probationer minister not forgetting the genuine kindness of his wife, Evelyn.

THE TALE END OF NORTH BELFAST

I have never felt more at home than when I am among what may be broadly called 'the working class' and the old North Belfast Mission and its pastoral community was full of them. Among those we got to know was a lady called Mrs. Meek, one of those mild-mannered friendly people it is always nice to meet. Just before we left Ireland for the Caribbean, Phyllis and I got a message that Mrs. Meek had cancer and was at her daughter's home and that she wanted to see us again. When we went to see

Mrs. Meek's gift tablecloth

her, she gave us the gift of a beautiful Christmas Tablecloth all embroidered by herself - a moving gesture from a dying lady. It has decorated our table every Advent and Christmas for over four decades until the present, and it prompts each year happy memories of Mrs. Meek, and many like her, such great friends.

The early 1970's were dark with hatred and division but for us those good people were the light that shone in the darkness.

The darkness can be dismal but it never puts God's light out.

ELEUTHERA

The route that would take us to the island of Eleuthera in the Bahamas went through Birmingham in the English West Midlands. Phyllis had always been quite strict with herself and with me, about the need to leave behind for others, a clean house. So we both worked all day on the Rathcoole Manse before catching the over-night ferry to Heysham. I can vividly remember how, when I had driven our little green mini car on board and we were up on deck just to look around, a shattering explosion went off nearby in the City Centre - what a typical farewell from the Belfast of 1973!

With two African Ministers at Kingsmead College

Next morning we drove to Holly Tree and our dear Auntie Dot, before going on to Kingsmead College in Selly Oak, Birmingham. There we spent six months on an orientation course to prepare for life in the Caribbean. The Principal was the Rev. Dr. Albert Mossley and our area Tutor was the Rev. Bruce Swapp. Bruce and Esme Swapp very quickly became close friends to us and they introduced us to parenthood as we babysat for them. Bruce was a Minister of the Methodist Church in the Caribbean and the Americas, a native of Jamaica and very knowledgeable about Caribbean life and culture.

We lived in a very cosmopolitan community with people from all over the world, and in a truly ecumenical situation with those from all branches of the Universal Church - Orthodox, Catholic and Protestant. The Mission Studies were stimulating and the cultural diversity exciting.

On the family front, the big event for us was the birth of Mark at the Queen Elizabeth Hospital, Edgebaston on 8th. March 1974. We had time to bring Mark home to Ireland and introduce him to his relations before flying to the Bahamas. I said to Phyllis on the trans-Atlantic flight to Nassau, "If anybody had told me five years ago that I would do this, I would have laughed at the very idea." There was an aspect of adventure about it all - and even a hint of foolhardiness!

The island of Eleuthera is around a hundred miles from North to South but only five miles at its widest point, and in most places on the island you can see the sea on both sides, its so narrow. There were ten churches in the South Eleuthera Circuit and I had pastoral charge of the five in the deep south of the island, with the Manse at Rock Sound. My Superintendent the Rev. Desmond Mason had charge of the five churches in the central part of the island and in addition had to carry the administration of the whole Circuit. The M.C.C.A. Conference had issued a Dispensation for me to administer Communion and of course I was baptising from my first Sunday onwards as well. I found it a bit daunting to find myself on my own at the Lord's Table for the first time and the Baptisms from unusual family structures, new to me then, were somewhat challenging for a while. The opportunity to preach and evangelise and exercise pastoral care was a dream come true.

I discovered that you can be lucky twice. I was still a Probationer Minister, that meant that the second phase of my training for ordination was still ongoing and I was under the supervision and direction of a Superintendent Minister. Desmond Mason was the perfect Superintendent for me, we just hit it off from the start and

A bunch of budding Missionaries at Kingsmead

Rev. Dr. Ronald & Mrs. Kezia Wilson, West African friends at Kingsmead

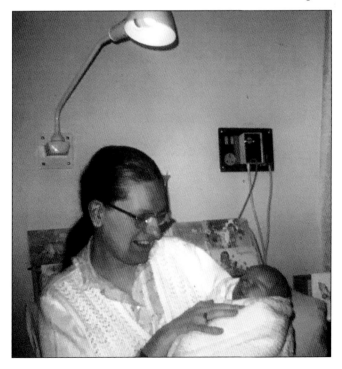

Phyllis & baby Mark at Queen Elizabeth Hospital, Birmingham

(L to R) Rev. Winston Graham, Rev. Bruce Swapp and myself

Rev. Desmond & Mrs. Kathleen Mason relaxing in our Harbour Island Manse

his wife Kathleen and their family were goodness incarnate to Phyllis, Mark and myself. Desmond was from St. Lucia in the South Caribbean and was a great combination of deep spiritual devotion, true humanity and exquisite humour. Another of my great privileges was to have worked alongside him for two years.

My Ordination Day arrived, a high moment in the life of any Minister. The President of the M.C.C.A. Conference, the Rev. Claude Cadogan, came specially from Antigua to preside, and although Phyllis and Mark were the only family present, I was surrounded by a Church Family which meant everything to me. The Rev Patterson Deane preached an unforgettable sermon that burned into my soul. Some of the best and most able Ministers I was ever to know were there - people like Edwin Taylor, Nymphas Edwards, J.T. Seymour and Eric Clarke.

I was twenty-nine years old on my Ordination evening and I had spent the previous ten years preparing for that climactic event in my life. Claude Cadogan was a towering figure, both physically and in terms of his leadership qualities and spiritual stature. I came away from my Ordination Service knowing that I was a Minister of the Church of Jesus Christ for ever! I was the only ordinand and no ceremony could ever be more effective than my Ordination.

That was in January 1976 and the same synod at which I was ordained, drafted me to be stationed in the North Eleuthera Circuit - my own Superintendency straight away! To be appointed as my own boss with charge of a significant Circuit in the Bahamas District and with my seat on the District General Purposes Committee, was indeed affirming. However I knew before I got there that this would be a great test of my fitness for the Methodist Ministry beyond the basic role of preaching and pastoral visiting, into the whole area of administration and management responsibility for finance and property. There were six churches in the North Eleuthera Circuit, located on four islands, involving me in a working life of boat travel and driving combined, the like of which I could only have vaguely imagined before going there!

My proneness to sea-sickness was not a problem as the journeys were so short that there was no time to get sick!! The Circuit area consisted of the Northern portion of the island of Eleuthera and three inhabited satellite islands. Three of my churches were on Eleuthera and the others each on one of the satellites and to complicate matters further, the main residential Manse was on one of the small islands, Harbour Island.

It all had an economic and political history, Harbour Island had its own Shipyard in the days of sail-driven wooden schooners and was the seat of local government. We had 'Mission Houses' or minor manses on Eleuthera, Current Island and Spanish Wells. There were other complexities beyond the merely geographical - racial division lived on from the colonial past.

Until the 1950's the Bahamas was the South Africa of the Caribbean with a strong practice of segregation and racial inequality and in this Circuit we had one church with an all-white congregation where a black Local Preacher had never stood in the pulpit. That church had split before my time when the Rev. Edwin Taylor, an excellent black Minister, preached there and a new independent evangelical congregation had been formed by the dissenters. The issues over Lay Preachers was not writ large in the same way but I felt strongly that it had to be faced. I decided to ask the Stewards to nominate to me two black Local Preachers they could accept and we started with them and after a couple of years we had all left the former prejudice behind us - at least with regard to the Circuit Preaching Plan.

John Wesley instructed our early Methodist predecessors never to be unemployed - and unemployment never remotely threatened me in North Eleuthera. I had Bible Classes, Local Preachers training and Confirmation Classes - with all the related preparation work. I had financial accounting for the six churches and the central account of the Circuit. Most of the Sunday offerings were simply put in paper bags off the plate and handed to me when I came on my quarterly round of Leaders' Meetings. For building work, I paid the tradesmen myself and at fundraising auctions I was the auctioneer. I had many Weddings, most of them from our local families but also of some tourist couples who wanted to get married in the islands. Some of the Funerals could be wonderful celebrations of a saintly life, with heavenly singing, but sadly some were the result of murder or suicide. I had adult and infant Baptisms - on one Easter Sunday twenty in all, one young lad getting the name of 'Leonardo DaVinci' and my last Funeral in the Bahamas was for one 'Joseph Stalin Bethel'.

Due to my constant travel round the four islands I was often asked to take merchandise such as straw work, honey or even locally made perfume, from place to place, and of course to bring back the payment! Coffins were among the items I dealt with in this way and people even sent their bank deposits with me as they had no local bank branch or facility for banking and it saved the small

With my Superintendent, Rev. Desmond Mason   Rev. Eric Clarke, District Chairman

My Ordination

shopkeeper the time and expense of travelling. I was constantly asked to speak to the Doctor, the Bank Manager or the Magistrate on behalf of those with problems to be resolved.

North Eleuthera was the sort of pastoral community where there always seemed to be some controversial matter to the fore at any given time. It could be a disciplinary question relating to a Lay Preacher or other Leader, a property dispute or simply a row over stray goats between two church members or the offence caused by the testimony given by someone in a court case.

I was thirty when I went there and I used to think that I would have needed the developed wisdom of a person twice my age to cope with the situations continually coming before me. It stretched me to the outer limits of my capacity for pastoral ministry but it left me strong.

In 1977, after a three year tour of duty, our Furlough came along -time to go back home for three months to rest. In Ardnagesson the big difference was that my Granny Jennie had died the previous year and mum was still in a deep grief over the loss of her mother. Mark, then three met all his grandparents in a meaningful way and we had a great time reconnecting with the home Church as well as with our family circles. My sister Charlotte's wedding was the highlight of it all, as I administered the vows between her and Willie Maye.

The old home was down to just two permanent occupants now, my Mum and Dad. Ade was married to Violet, and Irene to Walter Barclay. We all had our own homes in various places and our children were starting to make their presence felt in the widening family. The time soon came for us to return to North Eleuthera. On the day we were leaving the farm in Ardnagesson, one of the cows came in heat and Dad was away so I took her to the bull on a neighbouring farm before leaving. Mum's parting words to me were: "If you were here for the next three years, there would be jobs for you to do every day." That's farming!

Back to the complexities of North Eleuthera and to the absolute delight of working with our people there. Because of the topography of the place, I was away from home overnight about one third of the time. Thank God Phyllis had strong nerves and could cope well with the children at the Manse. She sewed and embroidered - even painted parts of the big 1840 Manse at Harbour Island.

Our big family event was the birth of Robert at the Princess Margaret Hospital in

Harbour Island Manse

Nassau on 29th March, 1978. At the time my former Principal at Cliff College, Howard Belben and his wife Jean were with us in the Circuit for Evangelistic Services and all-in-all it was a truly good period in our lives. We now had two sons and Phyllis' nurse's training and experience was a great asset to family life - not only at this stage but throughout all the years. Indeed, Phyllis was my secretary, book-keeper, manager of the Manse guesthouse and general background support. It is no exaggeration to record that without her I could never have coped with the multifarious demands of the North Eleuthera Circuit. I have often said that any young man looking for a wife should begin his quest by visiting the nearest Teaching Hospital as a nurse can usually take the strain better than most!

Next door to the Manse on Harbour Island lived the Doctor - who covered the same territory as I did. Across the street was the Health Clinic with the nurse's apartment upstairs. The nurse was Robert's godmother - Delrose Brown from Jamaica. Many were the nights Delrose got me out of bed to help get an emergency patient away by boat across the Harbour to the ambulance aeroplane, which would come to North Eleuthera Airport. The stories of those hair-raising journeys would fill a book by themselves! Delrose and Phyllis became very close friends and our friendship with her has proved lifelong. Another great Jamaican friend was Sister Olga Brooks-Smith of Wesley House, Nassau. Sister Olga, a gracious Deaconess, was our mother in the Bahamas; Phyllis lodged with her when Robert was born and we all boarded there when we were in Nassau - which was quite often.

As the end of our second tour of duty in the West Indies approached, Phyllis and I both felt that the time had come for us to return to Ireland. Mark would by 1980, have had two years of Primary education in the Bahamas and our general sense was that we had started our lives in Ireland, with all its opportunities and faults and we wanted our children to start their lives in our homeland too. Accordingly, arrangements were made for me to be stationed by the Irish Methodist Conference as from 1st. July 1980.

As Harvest Auctioneer I sell a pig!

A farmer friend in his orange grove

Church Harvest decorations in a fishing community

My sister Charlotte with husband Willie Maye on their wedding day

Robert's Baptism day with Rev. Clarke & his godparents

For some time I had the idea in my head that I would like to cross the Atlantic by ship - as Missionaries had done before airline flights. One means of doing that was on the Queen Elizabeth II - the famous Q.E.2. But upon enquiry, the cost instantly brought it home to me that such luxury was only for the rich and famous! Mission House in London would of course finance us to the equivalent of an air passage and we succeeded in finding a Polish Ship, the 'Stefan Batory', at the right price, sailing from Montreal to London. So the trick then was to plan an itinerary that would bring us to Montreal in time for the departure date.

Easter Sunday 1980 was my last day of preaching duty in North Eleuthera and we set out on a journey that would take us up through the Eastern region of North America. We travelled by Greyhound Bus, and stopped with various friends and relatives along the way - my connections in New Jersey and Phyllis' in New York etc. Our last stop was with the Hoilett family in Toronto - close Jamaican friends when we met in the Bahamas. On to Montreal by train, a taxi to the docks and so aboard the ship for London.

Poland was then a Communist country of the Eastern Soviet Bloc and there was an austere atmosphere abroad, aboard! All the crew had deadpan facial expressions all the time and never a smile was seen. But it was not oppressive, more disciplined than anything and Phyllis, Mark, Robert and I enjoyed the trip home by sea. As Mark was missing a term at school, he and I spent a couple of hours each day in the ship's library going over some educational materials we had brought along for the purpose.

In nine days we were at Tilbury Docks and London to do our Final Furlough business at Mission House, Marylebone Road and thence to Auntie Dot near Cliff College - our home in the North of England. A taste of what we were coming home to came at Manchester Airport. Every item in our large amount of luggage was searched by the security personnel in minute detail - even my Bible was leafed through to ensure that it was what it appeared to be! For some reason there seemed to be a suspicion that we couldn't be for real. When security were eventually finished with us, the airline staff refused at first to take all our baggage as it was over the normal allowance. By this time my patience was exhausted and I have to confess that I lost my cool. I made it clear that whatever happened I would not agree to leave some of our belongings behind - I would pay the cost of the excess and take it with us. Fortunately my less-than-ideal reaction proved productive and all our stuff was loaded at no extra cost but I realised later that the outcome could have been very different. We knew, as we took our seats on that flight, that we were on our way home to a security zone.

THE TALE END OF ELEUTHERA

Quite a few people from the North Eleuthera 'mainland' worked on Harbour Island as it was relatively active economically. Carpenters and labourers worked on the buildings and women were in the hotels and foreign-owned private homes. One such woman we got to know well was the sort of female you could meet anywhere in the Caribbean region - astute and smart about everything except her relationships with men! She had four or five children - each to a different father - and I had baptised some of them. She was unmarried, from Eleuthera and working on Harbour Island. It became obvious that one of the local

Dinner aboard ship in mid Atlantic, homeward bound

men had picked her up as a girlfriend and sure enough, she got pregnant yet again.

When she went into labour, Nurse Delrose Brown worked with her all day and overnight to no avail and the Doctor decided to arrange for her to be flown to Nassau. A millionaires yacht was anchored out in the Harbour with a helicopter on it and when the owner heard of the trouble ashore he offered to send the helicopter to take the distraught expectant mother across the water to the Airport - to avoid the distress of a boat. She was placed in an old rickety wheelchair and had to be taken down the hill to the dock to board the helicopter. No man willing to wheel her down the hill could be found - for fear of being regarded as the father of her baby - so Delrose, not for the only time, persuaded me to do the necessary. We got her into the helicopter and with much flying dust from the propellers, she was swished across the sea to the airport.

I returned to the Manse to eat a much delayed lunch and as we sat at the kitchen table, Phyllis informed me that she could see the same lady at the centre of the drama walking into the clinic! I simply couldn't believe it, as I thought that by then she should be in the air and well on her way to hospital in the city. I went to the clinic and there they were, mother and baby, and poor Nurse Delrose almost as exhausted as the mother. The American volunteer pilot who was the Manager of his family's hotel on the island, revved up the engine of his light aircraft preparing for the takeoff run, and the baby, dislodged from the womb by vibration, arrived!

PETTIGO and IRVINESTOWN

Back in Belfast and on in a few days to Donegal to re-connect with our families in both places, to open a bank account, buy a car and generally get ourselves established once again in Northern Ireland. I had some sort of urge to plant my own vegetables, and even though it was mid-May and slightly late, I proceeded to do so on the home farm at Ardnagesson. Dad was still cultivating potatoes as he had always done, so I had well- prepared ground at my disposal in which to plant carrots, turnips, onions and cabbage. I attended Conference in Bangor, meeting colleagues and friends and as we had no home apart from the Manse that went with my pastoral station, we had to wait until 1st. July to be housed in our own right.

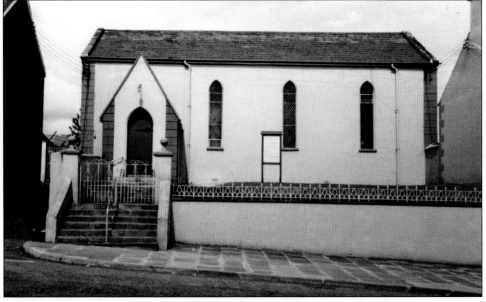

Irvinestown Methodist Church

Centenary of the 1882 Irvinestown Manse & Andrew's Baptism

We moved into the 1882 Manse in Irvinestown, and so I took up the work in the Pettigo and Irvinestown Circuit. The Circuit consisted of Tirwinney, Tullycherry, and Belleek as well as the two town churches and it was an amalgamation of the former Pettigo Circuit and the Irvinestown Circuit only a few years before. Those two Circuits each had two Ministers a couple of decades before and there tended to be a dependence on the Minister or the Minister's wife to run quite a few events, organisations and activities. In territorial terms I was covering ground where we had had four workers well within living memory. This actually impacted on Phyllis more than it did on me, because after all it was my main role in life to administer the work of the Church. Phyllis found herself running womens' organisations in the two main centres with women who were, on average, her mother's age.

I had duties during the mornings, afternoons and evenings most days and I preached at three or four Services on Sundays. It was definitely not the custom for any other voice to be heard except the Ministers - no Steward's announcements, readers or leaders in prayer. I had thirteen Harvest Thanksgiving Services to arrange, and when I 'phoned a colleague to ask for his help with the preaching, I discovered that he had twenty Harvest Services! The whole month of October was devoted to that theme and subject - which as a son of the soil, I liked.

I had three week-night Devotional Meetings with Bible Study and two or more School Assemblies per week. Life tended to be hectic, but my vegetable garden - reclaimed from a patch of nettles beside the Manse - was a great pleasure and relaxation and as a family we were very happy in Irvinestown.

Another feature of life in this period was the growing demands on both of us as Missionary Deputation Speakers. We stumbled into the awareness that nobody could be more popular in church circles than the 'new kid on the block' who has just returned from another part of the world.

At the end of our first year we realised that our children had had babysitters on two or three evenings almost every week throughout the Winter, as we were both out at so many speaking engagements. The babysitters were completely reliable, kind, good and willing to help us, but we both felt that we owed it to our own children to be with them more. Phyllis' appointments were mainly with womens' groups in all Protestant denominations, sometimes many miles away, necessitating a departure in the late afternoon to get to the venue. We agreed that we would carefully compare our diaries from here on and at least try to ensure that we would both be out in the evening only once per week.

Perhaps it is unreasonable to expect church members to appreciate how utterly difficult Manse or Rectory life can be and how hard it is to balance the needs of the work, and all its exciting opportunities, with a meaningful family life. Nevertheless we both greatly enjoyed sharing the story of the Caribbean Church with congregations and other groups all over Ireland for a period of at least ten years - as and when arranged.

At times I did feel that the whole culture of church life in Fermanagh was static and lifeless compared to the West Indies, with its much more spontaneous response. I was young and energetic and full of evangelical zeal in my mid-thirties and I sometimes thought that the reaction to most of my suggestions was a frowning caution. Given the cultural contrast, this was in no way surprising.

I was appointed as Synod Secretary and then as General Secretary of the Methodist Missionary Society (Ireland) so there was little spare time.

Our summer holidays from this station usually took the form of a stay in another Manse in the south of Ireland - preaching on the Sundays in exchange for accommodation. It enabled the local Minister to get away and as a family we very much enjoyed those times.

A good patch of grazing ground went with the Manse - the history of it going back to when the Minister travelled by pony and trap and kept the pony at the house. There was also a stable at the back of the house. When we arrived there were some ponies grazing on the Manse ground and a peppercorn rent was collected from their owner. I made it clear that I would make use of it myself. The following summer I bought two

My two store cattle

store cattle, grazed them for the summer and made a profit sufficient to purchase a freezer in which to preserve my own vegetables during the Winter. My family still had the freezer thirty years later - still in perfect working order!

Pastoral calls to the farms were a sheer delight and I could talk to the farmers and understand completely their working lives. I felt at home among my people in Fermanagh, Tyrone and parts of Donegal.

We had the excitement of our last addition to the family. Andrew was born on 15th. April 1982 in the Erne Hospital, Enniskillen. Phyllis got a part-time job at the Preschool Playgroup across the road. We were busy but somehow we could fit everything into our time that needed to be done - once we had learnt the hard way to control our commitments.

The youth organisations on the Circuit were outstanding, especially in Pettigo, such a small town divided by the Border. The Boys' Brigade and Girls' Brigade had remarkably strong numbers and in Mervyn Rowe and Marion Henderson we had excellent Captains - both assisted by very good Officers. It was my pleasure to be the Chaplain of both Companies for the four years we were there.

Olive Rowe ran a very successful Young People's Christian Endeavour Society in Pettigo, and Sally Simpson was her counterpart in Irvinestown.

If I had been required to contend with racism in the Bahamas, I could hardly be stationed on the Irish Border in the 1980's without encountering the sectarian divide. The Troubles were still raging in those years, with the Provisional I.R.A. engaged in a ruthlessly violent campaign against anybody associated with the

British security forces. Many of our members were in the Police and the Army - the Ulster Defence Regiment as it then was. The daily news bulletins contained frequent reports of such events as a bomb under a policeman's car, a machine-gun attack on a politician's family home or a young farmer shot dead while driving a tractor. In this dark atmosphere, it was hard to promote goodwill to all and reconciliation. But Phyllis and I felt strongly that we had a duty to do anything we could to reach across the barriers inherited from history.

For some years the Catholic women had faithfully attended the Women's World Day of Prayer Service in and around Pettigo but nobody had ever dared to make the move of holding the Service in the Catholic Church. When it was the turn of the Methodist Church to host the Service, Phyllis and I decided to use our good offices to initiate the move to the Catholic Church the following year. Although we sensed some reluctance, the move was made smoothly enough in committee terms. All seemed well until the time for the Service in the Catholic Church arrived, and in the surrounding weeks I ran into deep water over the whole arrangement. I had to sit through one church business meeting where I was castigated for heresy, my name was dragged through Orange Halls as a traitor and it was the only time that a colleague cancelled a speaking engagement on the grounds that I was certain to be verbally attacked and embarrassed if I came to that place.

Circuit Confirmation - my last Service in Irvinestown

The whole experience left me feeling like a fool and although I always try not to feel personally hurt by adverse events, this did wound me deeply. I was particularly annoyed when I was told that it was because I announced the service with too much enthusiasm that the whole trouble occurred. Apparently if I had read out the information clinically all would have been ok - my big mistake was to say that I hoped our women would take this opportunity to pray across the community divide.

The Troubles were raging and murders were tragically common in an atmosphere of political violence where that violence had become normal. One could only weep at the news of atrocities.

Mark was attending swimming lessons organised by Irvinestown Primary School, at the Leisure Centre in the Enniskillen Forum. His swimming instructor was a lively young woman and like all the children, Mark liked her very much. One evening she was getting a lift home with a policeman and an I.R.A. bomb exploded under the car. Both persons died instantly. I did not know the young lady but I still regard it as my worst personal moment of all those dreadful years, when my young son grabbed me and refused to let go, " Dad, I want you to tell me, why they killed her?" That was one of the days when my tears were bitter.

As I lived through those tense and difficult weeks over the World Day of Prayer controversy in Pettigo in the Spring of 1984, I was unaware that my days on that station were numbered. Generally speaking we were happy in West Fermanagh, being so close to my own native South Donegal - with such a similar culture and speaking accent. I felt completely at home and I was instructing a class of young people for Confirmation. I planted my Manse garden as usual, and I had bought in my usual two young cattle for the grazing fields. I was enjoying the bonus of living so near Ardnagesson that I could visit my parents fortnightly, either with Phyllis and the boys or on my own. Mum and Dad could also visit us and some of the happiest memories of our family history are of Christmas Days when Phyllis's parents were staying with us and my parents came as well to join in all the fun with our children.

I was aware that in the Methodist Ministry there can be such a thing as 'a Conference move,' and after four happy years in the Lakelands of Fermanagh, I was about to experience that very thing. I had been approached in the New Year confidentially about the possibility that I might be called upon to move, but nothing came of it and as I went to Conference in Dublin in June, I had an impression that the matter had been resolved without reference to me. But in

Dublin it emerged that the stationing complications of that year could only be resolved by making last-minute adjustments to the list of stations.

The consequence was that I returned home to Irvinestown with two weeks and two days to be in Ballynahinch. The normal sequence of events is that the whole process takes from October of the previous year, with various negotiations, proposals and drafts of the list during that time. Usually a Minister's family will know with reasonable assurance where they are going by February. It means that you can plan and pack and make arrangements with a remover etc.

In our case in 1984, with our three children, two of them at school, we just had to get on with it fast!

THE TALE END OF FERMANAGH

One of a Minister's privileges is the holy duty of taking the Lord's Supper to those no longer able to attend church, in their own homes. One day I drove along the country boreens near the Border, and up a long lane to administer Communion to an old lady in bed. I duly set out the bread and wine, said the appropriate words and gave her the elements, closing with the Benediction.

A very nice cat!

Returning to informal conversation as I packed the vessels away, I admired the lovely cat lying on top of the bed, fast asleep. The cat had outstanding markings of orange and black on a white background.

The communicant then put her hand inside her nightdress just under her breast, and withdrew a tiny newborn kitten, it's eyes still closed, with the comment, "Indeed she is a very nice cat and her wee baby is just like her."

And so it was - exactly!

BALLYNAHINCH

We arrived in the heart of Co. Down, among its hills and drumlins and kindly people, in July 1984. The move was sudden and I remember having a minor psychological reaction to it all, and feeling unwell for a few days when I was there about two weeks - the only time that ever happened to me on changing stations, but I was soon feeling fine.

One of the advantages of the new location was that I was much closer to Aldersgate House, University Road, Belfast, which made it much easier for me to carry out my work as General Secretary of the Methodist Missionary Society (Ireland). The Conference of 1983 had appointed me to that office and I had carried it out during my last year in Irvinestown, with long distances of travel for most of the duties concerned. I now started my new pastorate in Ballynahinch

Ballynahinch Methodist Church

knowing that I would have to integrate the work of M.M.S.(I) into the schedule of my new Circuit. It made for a busy, and to be truthful, an overcommitted life. For my first year I was external Superintendent of the Newcastle Circuit, with an excellent American Student Pastor, Morris Matthis, based in Newcastle.

With this went the Hospital Chaplaincies of Downpatrick, but Morris shared those responsibilities with me, and he was a willing worker - wise beyond his years.

Phyllis was a great support to me doing her bit as 'Minister's Spouse' in the church, taking up Marie Curie Nursing night duty and filling the gaps left in family life by my frequent absences from home. Without this backing I could not have managed to rise to the Secretaryship of M.M.S.(I). But this was the Conference remit that I really wanted. Academic achievements never really interested me - apart from the basic entry requirements for the Ministry, but I knew that this substantial part-time job would enable me to gain further understanding of the World Church and that through it I could build on my experience overseas. It meant taking responsibility for the Overseas Missionary business of the Irish Methodist Conference and dealing with matters related to the selection of candidates for overseas service. There were issues arising from those

Phyllis as a Marie Curie Nurse

working overseas and deputation plans to draw up for all of Ireland. I was a member of the Irish Council of Churches World Mission Committee, attending meetings in London around six times per year, and so the list of commitments went on.

But then, so far as the Stewards and members of Ballynahinch Methodist Church were concerned, I was their Minister and when it came to the on-going life of the local church in all its aspects, and urgent pastoral need, I had to do my best to keep the show on the road.

A Minister cannot say "Don't die on my day off," and neither can he say "Don't die when I have to go to Armagh or London for an important committee meeting." I loved and appreciated having my own pulpit and communion table and my Baptisms, Weddings and Funerals to fulfil, even though it meant burning midnight oil and rising very early from time to time. Preaching to the same congregation continually does demand much time in study and preparation on the part of the Preacher. But I was still in my thirties and early forties and had the health and energy for that dual working life and I felt that I was answering the call of God through it all. I often used to think, during those years, of an old circus act I once saw in Donegal, in which a performer stood with one foot on the back of each of two white ponies as they trotted side-by-side around the ring. I imagined that Ballynahinch Methodist Church was one of the ponies and M.M.S.(I) was the other and I was the precarious-looking, standing rider! I used to pray that I wouldn't fall off before this particular jaunt of my journey through life was over.

There were some great highlights of my tenure in office as Missionary Secretary; the Commissioning of new Missionaries (as they were then still called) were always great events, usually held in the person's or couple's home church. The year 1986 was a big year, the Bi-centenary of Dr. Thomas Coke's arrival at St. John's, Antigua. He had mission workers with him and was heading for Newfoundland, but was seriously blown off course. He arrived at St. John's early on Christmas morning to find a congregation of a thousand people, mainly slaves, and administered Communion to them, most of them taking the Sacrament for the first time. This was the fruit of the work of Nathaniel Gilbert, started in 1760 and Coke left some of his volunteers in the Caribbean to co-ordinate and expand the work. It proved to be a key moment in Methodist Missionary history, and in British and Irish Methodism, as well as in the Caribbean; we were marking two hundred years of Mission.

Two events of 1986 still stand out in my mind, the visit of the Rev. Edwin Taylor, to Ireland, and the Caribbean Youth Exchange.

Edwin Taylor had been instrumental in our going to the Caribbean in 1974, in that he was Chairman of the Bahamas District and when he heard my name, he decided to take a chance with someone he had never met, and to say that I would be welcome in the Bahamas. So by the Grace of God that very positive phase of my early years in ministry unfolded. By 1986 Edwin was President of Conference of the Methodist Church in the Caribbean and the Americas, and now it was my turn to exercise my good offices to invite him to Ireland.

Bishop Armando Rodregiz of Cuba & his
interpreter Marianna Phillips

A Caribbean Candlelight Service

Caribbean Youth Exchange team on return visit 1987

Visit of Rev. Edwin Taylor, President of the Methodist Church in the Caribbean & the Americas

Christian Aid lunch

Our dormobile with donkeys at Achill Island

Boys at caravan on summer holiday

I met him at the airport and he lodged with us at the Ballynahinch Manse - as ever the life and soul of the party with our boys. He gave an outstanding series of Bible Studies at our Irish Conference in Donegal Square, Belfast - the sort of devotional expositions that fed into the Conference Agenda and resonated with the business in hand in a highly unusual way. In addition to that, the Mission Meeting, one of the main evening events of the Conference, was the Commissioning of a Team of Young People and Leaders to go to the Caribbean that summer. Again Edwin gave one of those brilliant public addresses of which he was always capable. He preached on the Sunday in Ballynahinch, cutting a striking figure with his deep African black complexion and dressed in white robes and it was no ordinary service. It struck me as I left him back to the Airport, what a telling impact he had made on our Conference and Church - he had brought the World Church, which has grown out of all our historic missionary efforts, back to us in person. Such is the way of life and the call of duty, that we were never to meet in person again.

Through my contacts with the wider Church, other visitors who graced my pulpit in Ballynahinch, included the Rev. Eric Clarke, Edwin's successor as President of the M.C.C.A.; Bishop Rodriguez, Head of the Methodist Church in Cuba; my former Superintendent in Eleuthera, the Rev. Desmond Mason and the Rev. Dr. Kenneth Greet, once Secretary and President of the British Methodist Conference. I was also able to introduce a form of worship service from the West Indies, during the Advent Season, the Caribbean Candlelight Service. Basically it is simply the lighting of seven candles after the reading of each of seven Scripture Lessons in turn, with a candlelight procession and recession etc. This proved to be the best attended Service of the year, both in Ballynahinch and later in Glengormley.

The second significant happening for me in 1986 was the Caribbean Youth Exchange. We selected one young person from each of our eight Districts in the Methodist Church in Ireland, and the Rev. Winston Graham, Treasurer of M.M.S.(I) and I led the Project, along with Mrs. Sandra Ker and Miss Jennifer Kingston. We visited the Bahamas, Haiti and Antigua and on our return home raised funds for a Nursery School facility in Nassau, Bahamas. Because I had been stationed in that part of the world, I had a particular responsibility for this whole exercise, which I greatly enjoyed. Winston and all our Team members were just brilliant and the whole experience was inspiring. My friend, the Rev. Dr.

Nymphas Edwards led a Return Team to Ireland in 1987 - another outstanding short period for all concerned.

All my five years as General Secretary for World Mission in the Irish Conference were challenging and fulfilling, but it was hard to ride the two ponies! I took the golden opportunity in 1988 upon the retirement of the Rev. Leslie Wallace, a missionary legend in his own right, from Sierra Leone, to hand over the Secretaryship to him and nobody could have been better fitted for that office.

When I went off on the Youth Exchange in 1986, I left the Rev. Alan Hanna, an active retired Minister, in pastoral charge of Balynahinch during my absence. Sadly he had to bury a young U.D.R. soldier murdered by the I.R.A., in a very high profile media-featured Funeral. The harsh reality of Northern Ireland during the Troubles was never far away. From time to time I found myself sitting with business or police families - sometimes until the small hours of the morning - because they had been threatened by the ruthless operators of political violence - Republican or Loyalist. Any Protestant church seen as liberal, ecumenical or pro-Catholic was regarded by Loyalist extremists as suspect and could be attacked physically and I was aware of a low level of threat all the time.

I had the privilege and challenge of being the Secretary/Co-Ordinator of the Billy Graham Livelink Mission 1989 for the Downpatrick Leisure Centre venue. A wide range of broadly evangelical churches participated in this effort, including a prayer group in the Catholic parish of Downpatrick. Many new commitments of faith in Christ were made, and it was all very exhilarating. Paisleyite opposition was inevitable and I found myself on the 'phone with B.B.C. producers and presenters in London when I came home from the Mission, as our detractors knew how to get attention! But God had a sense of humour, because the only two persons who responded to the appeal to come forward on the first evening, were one a Roman Catholic and the other a Free Presbyterian!

Despite all the conflicting demands of life, Ballynahinch was an ideal place for me at this stage of my career in the ministry. My predecessor, Harold Good had established a socially open atmosphere which I very much liked and I found a ready welcome for my evangelical message among the people. There were quite a few families at the same stage as us - the parents and children similar to Phyllis and myself and our boys in terms of age, and this made for much commonality.

We started an ecumenical Christian Aid Lunch on Thursdays, (Market Day) in our Methodist Halls, with teams from various churches working in turn to deliver it. Our menu was basic - just the soup and cheese type - but I used to joke that we were the only eatery in town with a Medical Doctor on the staff! One of our Methodist volunteers was a Doctor in her early child- rearing years and on a break from Medicine. We had plenty of customers and good fellowship and we raised thousands of pounds for Christian Aid. I was a 'go-for' and waiter most weeks.

All told I was surrounded by the very best of Leaders. Valerie Crawford was excellent as Sunday School Superintendent and John Unsworth equally great as Youth Leader. John Charles was a dream as Organist and it was with real personal sorrow that I had to bury John after only three years working together - though I felt that I had known John all my life. My friend Wesley Unsworth then became organist and was also a true co-worker.

My first experience of broadcasting a service live on radio with the B.B.C. came at Ballynahinch. My college classmate, the Rev. Dr. Bert Tosh was based in the B.B.C., Belfast, in the Religious Programmes Department and he recruited me for this role. One thing I failed to foresee was that a fair proportion of my congregation stayed at home to listen to the Service on the radio! After my first time round with this in 1985, I suffered from a migraine headache for the only time in my life. It nearly wrecked my nerves and I spent the next day in bed taking painkillers when I should have been off with the family on holidays, but I had recovered by the next day and we got away in our old-banger dormobile.

It was Charlie Bain who told me that a caravan is the best kind of holiday arrangement for a Minister and family and as so often he proved to be right. After one year with the old dormobile, which was not a good investment, we moved to a caravan and never looked back.

I inherited a growing church in Ballynahinch - the demographics were in our favour, with so many families moving out of Belfast to live in such a pleasant countryside. The congregation numbered around two hundred on a good day and I had the pleasure of confirming new members several times - once when all eleven candidates were people in their forties.

We had to be active in fundraising to pay for the brilliant suite of buildings, and catering for groups from other churches was one of the methods for this. It kept

Phyllis and the ladies of the church busy, and with only one family car, we often had to engage in fast turn-arounds. But one of our positive assets was my Aunt Lily Hagan and her family at their farm out the road at Cargycreevy. Lily and my female cousins were ready babysitters any evening - and many were the times they helped us.

I had been hoping to concentrate more on my pastoral work in Ballynahinch when I relinquished the Secretaryship of M.M.S.(I) in 1988, but that year the Spring Synod elected me as District Stationer - their representative on the Conference's Stationing Committee. This involved a good deal of travel and whole days spent on concentrated

Aunt Lily Hagan as a young woman

committee work. The following year they nominated me as Chairman of the Down District as that office was then named - so I was one of the Bishops of Irish Methodism! But I was soon disabused of any notion that my star was rising fast - for I was immediately drafted for a change of station that would take me out of that District and out of this new-found high office that went with it.

A confirmation group at Ballynahinch

THE TALE END OF BALLYNAHINCH

I first met Bob McNiece at the Dublin Conference in 1984 - the week that my sudden move to Ballynahinch was made - so we had plenty to talk about right away. Bob was a diminutive man with a most likeable personality and a deep and sincere faith. When he prayed with me in the vestry before a Service, I always felt that Jesus Christ was standing in the room with us.

It was a tragic shock to Bob and his family, and to the whole community, when his youngest son was killed in a road accident on the Sunday afternoon of my first Harvest Thanksgiving Weekend in Ballynahinch. Bob was a widower, his wife having passed away after a long battle with cancer several years before, leaving him to finish the rearing of his family of sons, on his own. Trevor was the youngest at fourteen, a typical lively lad helping our local milkman and jumping with energy.

It was one of those Funerals that focused the grief of the town and surrounding district. Four hundred young people at Ballynahinch High School made it clear that they were all going to attend Trevor's Funeral and the seating capacity of our church was slightly over two hundred. The Vice-Principal of the school asked me to come for a Special Assembly before the church service. It was an appropriate act of worship, a short devotion with intense concentration, the large congregation of youngsters hanging on my every word.

Bob was a Crossing Warden at the High School and all the students loved him dearly. Such was the effect of the tragedy - combined with the quality of Bob's Christian example - that a whole new movement of Christian fellowship developed in the school over the following years. It was the most striking example of a fruitful Christian witness and of positive good growing out of disaster, that I ever knew.

GLENGORMLEY

I n going to Glengormley in 1990, I succeeded the Rev. Winston Graham, by this time my closest friend and confidant in the Irish Methodist Ministry. The station had taken a heavy toll on Winston's health and I knew that it could have the same effect on me.

At that stage Glengormley was arguably the largest congregation in the Irish Conference with two Sunday morning services and with 670 known families affiliated - and many more kept popping up in times of extreme need. I would be contacted urgently about someone in Intensive Care after an accident, but there would be no trace of them or their family on our extensive pastoral records. My policy was to help whoever I was asked to help regardless of their previous association, or lack of it, with the church. I had at least two thousand souls in my

Glengormley Methodist Church

pastorate and I was faced each week with more need than I could hope to meet. My hospital visiting list for a week could be up to twenty patients in five hospitals.

One of the pastoral rules I have always tried to follow is to visit anyone due for surgery, the evening before the operation. The main battle was always obtaining the information about the whereabouts of ones parishioners rather than the making of the visits. This became progressively harder for parish clergy as data protection law fed into the culture of hospital chaplaincy. By the time I retired hospital chaplains no longer routinely informed pastors that their congregants were in hospital, as legally they needed the express consent of the patient to do so. This whole trend started in the 1990s, thus making pastoral information hard to get.

Crises came in quick succession; suicide, terminal diagnosis, termination of pregnancy, marital breakup, addicts arriving at the church in the evening demanding, with menaces, to see the Minister - the list of crying need was endless. I often had two or three meetings in an evening, carefully timed to accommodate my attendance, but scheduled appointments could be interrupted at any time by pastoral emergencies. I was called out from time to time during the night.

If there is one profession which looks easy but is in reality difficult, it is the pastoral ministry and I found that in Glengormley the struggle was made harder by the relatively large number of people to whom I had to respond. Ministers should never think that they ought to be unaccountable or beyond scrutiny, but it has to be said that criticism of the pastor can at times be cheap and superficial.

Those who feel frustrated or disillusioned with their own lot in life - such as the unhappy retired - can sometimes turn on their minister irrationally. There were moments when I felt that there was little appreciation, on the part of a small hardcore of inveterate critics, of the fact that I worked fourteen-hour days and had little hope of a clear day off per week, and that it was not unusual for me to have a Wedding and Funeral on the same day, two Weddings on a Saturday or three or four Funerals in one week.

Inevitably there were those who felt neglected and there was attention-seeking leading to negative rumour all the time. I have to confess that my pastoral task was simply humanly impossible and I threw myself at it too hard for my own good in my first few years there.

The other major problem I had, related to the theological diversity of the church.

There were many whose concept of the church was firmly traditional, middle-of-the-road Protestantism - familiar hymns sung to well-worn tunes and accompanied by the church organ, being the main liturgical feature. Many others, largely as the result of Charismatic Renewal, had moved on from that to lively praise songs sung to guitars, drums and wind instruments.

On the traditional side, we had the Church Choir, and on the modern side, we had Glengormley Methodist Youth Choir, led by Jack Audley and famous for their lively praise carried on a bus throughout Ireland, with tours in England and the U.S.A. There was tension between these two worship styles; with very strong partisan views on both sides - and everybody looked to the Minister to provide their preferred culture.

We had a top-class Girls' Brigade Company, with Barbara Lowry as Captain, succeeded in my time by Ann McDowell - who continued to lead the Company with great success for many years. Much to my delight, we had a good Boys' Brigade Company led by John McFarland as Captain and then succeeded by Ken McFaul, in my time. Robert Laughlin stands out in my memory as a B.B. Officer of utter dedication and faithfulness.

The Methodist Womens' Association, as it was then called, was strong in numbers and ethos and the Young Womens' Association served younger ladies. I had a joke in those days, not much appreciated by Phyllis, that she and Rosemary Audley were in the young womens' group in Rathcoole in 1972, and they were still young women in 1992!

Barbara Lowry, a senior Nurse Manager, assisted Phyllis in applying for nursing work and this resulted in part-time employment with Marie Curie Cancer Care and at Abbots Cross Medical Practice Treatment Room.

A monthly Men Only Meal and Meeting provided fellowship for men in a very positive Christian way - ably led by Alan Strong.

We had Christian Endeavour for children and young people and when Paul Nesbitt joined the church, he brought to that branch of our work, his experienced leadership and marked development.

The Friendship Club met monthly - mainly couples in middle life - and Phyllis and I greatly enjoyed those informal and good-humoured meetings.

The new Wesley Manse, Glengormley

Girls Brigade flower arrangement
at festival 1990

Boys Brigade flower arrangement
at festival 1990

Holly the collie

Holly inspires sermon preparation

Our family in the Manse

Mark & Cathy on their wedding day

Ulster Project group in Texas

A very good Mother and Toddler group was started in our time by Linda Barnes, Heather Smith and Michelle McCloy - soon attracting new young families to the church.

It was all very exciting and there was never a dull moment night or day, but with all these organisations and their variety of emphasis and culture, tensions used to arise quite often over the use of the church halls and who or what should have precedence or priority. Private Birthday Parties would sometimes be arranged on the back of a nod from someone in the church, complete with Bouncy Castle etc., all set up in the main hall where such a standard event as the B.B. Display was to be held. The Minister was seen as the ultimate arbiter in all cases of dispute, and I could come home from hospital visiting around 9pm to word that I was urgently needed at the church. This was before mobile 'phones became universal and looking back I think that on balance it was better I didn't have one then!

Life was far from easy, but Glengormley was the greatest pastoral and preaching opportunity I could have wished for. I was supported by some of the best Lay Leaders I ever knew and I used to tell them that amidst all the range of life and activity in and around the church, there was one thing we were always doing, and that was evangelising - telling the Gospel story and hoping and praying for a response. I worked on an open attitude to Baptisms, Weddings and Funerals and I got plenty of the 'rites of passage' work to do. I have always felt that the best way to follow the Galilean Ministry of Jesus is to be as open to all as possible. I am glad to say that throughout my ministry, and especially in Glengormley, I saw many people come through to faith in Christ after being helped pastorally in a time of need. Most notably after I helped by presiding at a Funeral, one or two from the family would become part of the congregation and respond to the Christian message and this was a frequent experience.

At the end of my first year in Glengormley, I put it to my Leaders on an 'Away Day' that we should plan a major Evangelistic Outreach Mission at the church. After reflection and prayer they agreed and we took two years to move the entire programme of the church to converge into one event lasting eight days in October 1993. We invited the Rev. Martin Turner, then of St. Alban's, later of Methodist Central Hall, Westminster, to come as the Preacher. That week proved to be a true highlight in the ongoing life of the church, with excellent drama and music and an atmosphere of prayer and expectation. Many came to saving faith, and many renewed their Christian commitment and the spirituality of the congregation was enhanced with a fresh confidence. In the weeks that followed, I found myself visiting numerous families newly contacted.

Drusilla Cunningham was Organist when we arrived in Glengormley and so began a friendship with Phyllis and myself that would last long. She was succeeded by Richard Topping - at first as a Strandmillis student, but soon to become a Teacher and Headmaster. Richard used to remind me of John Charles in Ballynahinch, a natural musician to the fingertips and always ready to play anything. His contribution to the life of the church was incalculable. Having someone of Richard's caliber meant that we could broadcast services with the B.B.C confidently - on one occasion reaching thirty million listeners on the World Service. I got letters and postcards afterwards from all over the world!

In February 1994, I had the greatest health trauma and scare of my life. I had a minor heart attack, diagnosed after the event and my only time in hospital was overnight for a test. The Cardiologists sent me on my way with a few serious instructions about workload, lifestyle, diet and exercise and I finished my career without looking back in terms of general health.

The adoption of our rescue dog Holly, the Border Collie, was a definite part of my therapy. She used to be 'star of the show' at my five school assemblies in and around Glengormley, and at many a Children's Day Service all over the place. Her obedience training proved perfect and she never put a foot astray or let me down in public.

I had to face opposition in Glengormley the like of which I never encountered anywhere else, which meant that I learnt more about the politics and dynamics of a church, or any human community, during this time than I did during any other period. It was knowledge that would stand me in good stead later when I was called upon to lead and mentor my colleagues in ministry. I was to discover that I was by no means the only pastor to face conflict and negative drag along the way in the service of Christ, and I was better able to listen, advise and help because I had been through hard times myself.

It would only be dishonest not to record the ugly as well as the pretty, the nasty as well as the nice, but nothing could ever have taken away my overwhelming sense of the opportunity of a lifetime and the power of God the Holy Spirit that

I felt throughout my eight years in Glengormley. It was the only station I was to occupy for the maximum period allowed by the ordinary rules of our Conference at that time. Dorothy Boyle was Secretary of the local church's governing body - then the Leaders' Meeting - efficient and able and with her working background in a Trade Union, she was an invaluable friend and wise counsellor.

On the family front, good things happened for us at Glengormley: Phyllis and I celebrated our 25th. Wedding Anniversary with a holiday in Jersey in 1997.

Mark and Cathy Edwards met, singing the praises of God in the Youth Choir, leading to Marriage and a family. Mark moved on from Methodist College to Queen's University to read Law and then to Manchester for a Master's Degree in International Business and on to London to qualify as an Accountant.

Robert and Debbie Redmond met and formed a lasting relationship as well, leading to Marriage and a family. Robert went from Glengormley High School to the University of Ulster, Jordanstown, to study Informatics which would take him into a career in Information Technology. Andrew too, came through Glengormley High, a convenient walking distance from our Manse, to G.C.S.E. at the age of sixteen, just as we were ready to leave.

I first met with the Ulster Project at Glengormley. It was started by a Church of Ireland Rector in the 1970's and its main activity is to take equal numbers of Catholic and Protestant young people from Northern Ireland to America for a month in the Summer. Both Robert and Andrew went to Arlington, Texas when they were the right age, and in Robert's case the Simon family became lifelong friends. Through the good offices of Ken Simon, Robert spent his third university 'year out' in Texas with the Fidelity financial company. It gave him an edge and and positive C.V., that took him into computer software engineering at a time of downturn in the industry - and he never looked back.

In October 1997, a desire that had been in my heart for thirty years was fulfilled. I had always wanted to host an evangelistic team from Cliff College, it took three decades, but eventually it happened. They worked and witnessed in our church, church halls and in the five schools I myself visited, for a very effective week of youth outreach.

I always knew that 1998 would be my year of departure from Glengormley and to tell the truth I was somewhat tired and in need of a change of scene by the time that year came along. I was, and still am, grateful to God and the Methodist Church for allowing me the chance to serve in such a diverse and demanding pastoral charge. It gave me the opportunity to exercise my ministry to the fullest possible extent, and I can say that I gave it my best effort.

For six of those eight years, my 'senior curate' was the Rev. Billy Nichol- like my Stewards and so many others, a great support. Billy was the Minister with whom I worked closely for the longest period of time and I felt truly honoured a decade later, to be invited by his wife Jean and their family to give the eulogy at his Funeral, in 2007.

THE TALE END OF GLENGORMLEY

When visiting a house one day, I found myself sitting in an armchair when a large red rooster walked in and hopped onto the arm of the chair. The householder gave me a slightly gruff warning: "Watch him, yer ruuverence, for he would pick the eyes out a ye."

A Red Rooster

I have often told this story to friends and asked them to guess where I was working when I had that earthy experience. Some had said Donegal and others the West Indies, but I was in Queens Park Estate in Glengormley. The old country instincts can come in handy anywhere!

MOUNTPOTTINGER

To say that Mountpottinger presented me with a change of working context would be an understatement, it was more to be described as a contrast. Built in Ballymacarrett in the heart of East Belfast in 1887, just as Queen Victoria had made the town a City, Mountpottinger Methodist is nineteenth century free church architecture at its best. It has the usual high pulpit, rounded gallery, symmetry of design, perfectly finished and polished hardwood

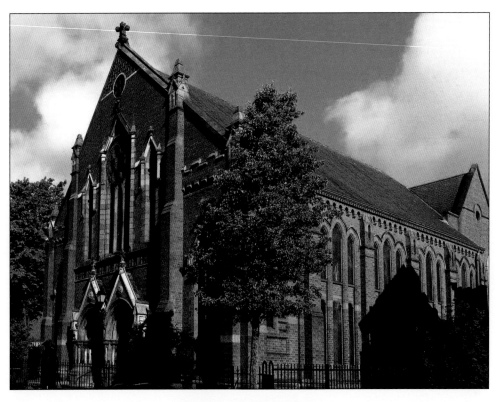

Mountpottinger Methodist Church

that characterised the public buildings of that imperial period.

It would be easy to think of disadvantages such as the inflexible fixed pews, the pulpit too remote, the danger of a mere museum conveying a message of the dead past instead of the living present, but I found

Mountpottinger internal sanctuary

that I felt strangely at home in Mountpottinger from my first Sunday there. In a sense this was surprising, for I have always been a country person at heart and this was the inner city. Furthermore, I had just come from the vibrant outer suburbs of Newtownabbey and here life was much more settled and predictable. However the church was united and well co-ordinated, with the sort of leadership team that could easily have managed a much larger church - an advantage of the long history was maturity. Call it a dying culture if you wish, but I enjoyed the High Wesleyan tradition of this church, especially the manner in which it presented me with the opening to preach my heart out every Sunday morning and so fulfil my calling.

I was now serving a pastoral community only about a quarter the size of Glengormley and that in itself made my life much more liveable. Socially, I used to describe Mountpottinger as a village in the city, as the people knew one another well and news travelled amongst them with lightening speed. A great asset of this was that I found myself to be part of a first- class informal pastoral team, mainly of women, constantly on the move visiting. All I had to do after the Bible Study lesson on a Wednesday evening was to listen and note what I heard in the prayer requests and I knew immediately who needed my attention most. It meant that I was never the first or only person from the church to visit anybody; if I called on someone in hospital, they would invariably have been visited by one or two of those faithful women working together. I found that it was a very positive experience to be the pastor of a pastoral community.

John Kelly as Steward and Ian Brown as Treasurer were both excellent. Vivienne Brown then became Steward and gave me great support with worship and we were able over time to move our worship towards a more youth-friendly culture. Davy Catherwood was ideal as Boys' Brigade Captain, Sylvia Hynes and later Helen Beggs were great leaders of the Girls' Brigade and Margaret Robinson led the Girl Guides so very well - in addition to her role as Society Steward. Once again, I was blessed with the Church Organist of my dreams in Margaret Spence - musically competent, flexible and always so helpful.

Much was to happen in our family whilst at 'the Mount' and this fellowship of faith helped us through it all.

Phyllis and I became property owners for the first time when we bought a small old fisherman's cottage in the village of Ballyhalbert on the Ards Peninsula. It was to be a quiet retreat and holiday resort for many years. As you ate your breakfast on a clear day, you looked across the Irish Sea to Scotland.

We were back in Glengormley on 28th. December 1998 for the Wedding of Mark and Cathy, and I felt deeply moved as I administered their vows. Despite the Boxing Day Storm, which threatened the whole travel arrangements, everybody got there and we all had a great day to remember.

Phyllis' mother Susan, like myself born in Ardnagesson, had been unwell for years and passed away in April 1999. It meant much to us that she was well enough to go with us once into our lovely Mountpottinger Church. It was not the time of a service but we read a favourite passage for Susan from the Pulpit Bible and she was delighted to see our new spiritual home.

My brother, Ade, took ill in the Autumn of 2000; it soon became a diagnosis of terminal cancer, and he died in April 2001. It was a very hard and tragic time for his wife Violet and the family and for us all. It was particularly difficult for my parents, old and in failing health themselves, to watch their son suffering and moving towards his death. Ade had started his working life as a mechanic and

Our Ballyhalbert Cottage

succeeded in business with his own garage and at the age of 53, he was gone from this life. It caused me to pass through a profound emotional trauma, from which I have never completely recovered. By staying close to the Cross, my faith remained strong, but my heart was sore and broken.

Phyllis' brother, the Rev. Canon Jim Harron had lost his first wife Ellen, in 1997 in a very similar way to Ade's early death, and again the cause was cancer. After five years, in 2002, he married the Rev. Elizabeth Mayes, a retired Methodist Minister. I revelled in the role of Best Man as Archdeacon Ken Good presided in Shankill Parish Church, Lurgan. Ken got a phone-call as we signed the papers in the vestry - the Archbishop of Armagh - to tell him that he was elected as Bishop of Derry and Raphoe! I was the first to make a public announcement about it at the Wedding Reception.

The next big day was the Wedding of Robert and Debbie on 12th. October, 2002 in Mountpottinger Methodist Church. I presided and then walked down the aisle with Debbie's Mum, Frances, in my other role as the groom's father. Some of the guests who didn't know me were heard to remark that Bob's dad was a 'dead ringer' for the Minister!

Another sad occasion was the death of my father in the Spring of 2005. Illness and old age had simply led to the situation whereby Dad's life was over and he passed away. On my Dad's last birthday 10th. November 2004 our first grandchild was born. Cathy gave birth to Layla, a lovely little girl, and I really felt that life was moving on.

Mountpottinger was good to us throughout all those joys and sorrows, patient with my necessary absences during Ade's illness and at other times - totally supportive and uncomplaining. I have often told my family and friends that the nicest job I ever had was to be minister of Mountpottinger Methodist Church.

In my last three years in Mountpottinger I was the Belfast District Superintendent, quite demanding in itself, but I was so happy in 'the Mount' that I scarcely felt any strain at all in fulfilling everything required of me in that office.

My friend from the Cliff College days, the Rev. Robert Russell, then General Secretary of M.M.S. (Ireland), asked me to undertake the chairmanship of the Stricklands Missionary Conference, the annual gathering of Irish Methodists, in the interest of World Mission. During my tenure, we managed to change the venue

Jim & Elizabeth Harron's wedding reception

Robert & Debbie on their wedding day.

Phyllis & I with the Lord Mayor & Lady Mayoress of Belfast - Jim & Greta Rodgers

The Lord Mayor's reception for friends & family

and expand it into the Global Vision Conference, with a multiplied attendance.

Although our congregational life was peaceful and happy, East Belfast could still be disturbed and violent during this period. The sectarian interface with the Short Strand, combined with the Drumcree trouble which plagued the Province for a decade each summer, meant that in my early years we had rioting in Ballymacarrett. Sometimes the traffic lights outside our church were burnt to charred remains. I was just fortunate that no Wedding or Funeral had to be carried out under such conditions.

I had the pleasant extension of my pastorate to include the Lord Mayor's Chaplaincy - being invited by my friend, and Mountpottinger member, Councillor Jim Rodgers, to be his chaplain when he was elected Mayor. I was also to be Jim's chaplain during his second Mayoralty and chaplain to Councillor

My in-laws - Oswald & Susan Harron

Wallace Brown (later Lord Belmont) when he was Lord Mayor. Civic occasions and formal dinners at the City Hall were a long way from Ardnagesson, but Phyllis and I enjoyed meeting so many interesting people. Human need is basically the same for us all, high or low, foreign dignitaries, cabinet ministers, or the drivers who transported them to their important engagements.

This was my last church that my parents would visit, and the last period when I would enjoy good times with them both on my visits to Donegal.

I left Mountpottinger in 2005 with the confidence that my colleague, Colin Duncan, Minister of Bloomfield Methodist Church, would lead the Mountpottinger and Bloomfield Circuit into a positive future.

THE TALE END OF MOUNTPOTTINGER

At our Wednesday evening meeting, I was informed that in a few days one of our members would be 90. So on the day I went to her home all prepared to administer Communion to her. When she opened the door and asked me my business, I wished her a Happy Birthday and explained that I would like to share the Lord's Supper with her.

The unexpected reaction was "well it's not very convenient , could you give it to me here?" It was obvious that I was not going to be admitted to the house, so my mind went into overdrive on the subject of what to do. It was a pleasant morning in May, the sun was shining and the birds singing, and I thought that if the Padres can do this on the battlefield, surely I can do it here. So I set out the elements on a low wall, said all the relevant words, gave the lady Communion and departed.

At home, Phyllis was surprised to hear what had happened and on the following Wednesday the members of that group were wide-eyed over it as well. One devout lady was determined to get to the bottom of what she regarded as an insult to the minister! The following Wednesday, she returned with a report. When confronted about the matter, the old woman had said, "I don't know what Mr. McElhinney has done to himself, I didn't recognise him at all, I thought he was a burglar come to rob the house."

Pretend plumbers and electricians are common, but has anybody in the criminal fraternity thought of the pretend pastor offering Holy Communion?

THE PRESIDENCY

I had been elected to office in the church before - to head the Down and Belfast Districts and as General Secretary of M.M.S. (Ireland.). Indeed the Missionary Secretaryship was the only Connexional position I would have felt disappointed not to get - that was my one ambition. As for any other high office, I had no desire to rise through the ranks at all.

In 2005, the Conference had me lined up for what looked like my last stationing move. I was drafted for Joanmount in Upper North Belfast, under the shadow of the Cave Hill. I was quite pleased about this as I would succeed the Rev. Dr Jim Williamson, who had taught me the rudiments of ministry in Donegal, and as my career in the

Methodist Conference Edinburgh Commemorative Tartan & Mug

ministry after college had started at the old North Belfast Mission just down the road from Joanmount.

I had been nominated for the Presidential vote at Conference 2004 and had polled strongly, so I knew that my name would appear on the ballot paper again in 2005. It came as a shock when it was announced that I was elected. I withdrew to the vestry of the Conference Church, Thomas Street, Portadown, to 'phone Phyllis at her workplace - Abbots Cross Medical Practice. When she answered I couldn't speak as I was overcome with emotion. After a pause I was able to tell her.

We were faced with the task of moving to Joanmount in the knowledge that after only one year I would effectively have a year out of that church. Not only that, but the demands of preparation for the Presidency, committee membership etc., would be such that I could not give Joanmount my undivided attention even in this initial year.

My Dad had died in April and Phyllis' father Oswald Harron was by this time, living with us and had taken seriously ill in the early summer. Pop Harron was great company and I had a close relationship with him. It was hard to see him so weak, but he did come home - though to another house - the Joanmount Manse.

In terms of both family and career, we faced demands and challenges as never before. But Joanmount gave me every possible support as I sought to prepare for, and rise to, the Presidency.

The Circuit Stewards, Daphne Lambe and Nigel Browne, and the voluntary Pastoral Assistant, Albert Morton, were superb in their help. I was also very fortunate in getting a retired colleague and good friend, the Rev. Sam Allen, as my Assistant and effective deputy in Joanmount for the Presidential year. Sam became the acting minister of Joanmount and I could go on my way around Ireland and the world, with an easy mind with regard to my normal pastoral and preaching duties. 2006/2007 was a whirlwind year in my life and in the life of our family.

Robert and Debbie were blessed with their first chid, the lovely Lily, just before I came into office. Cathy was near to her delivery date and bravely attended my Installation. Mark read a Lesson, and Honor was born shortly afterwards. My two dear sisters read Lessons and my Mother was there, no doubt with long thoughts and memories as she sat quietly through a long Service. Magees of Donegal made and donated my Presidential scarf - undyed wool to represent my shepherding life and employment with Magees. Peter Sweeney with whom I worked at Magees was there along with a minibus load of old Donegal friends, including Bill Scott my former B.B. Officer, Alicia Duncan (formerly Miss Kee) and Dr. Dick Kingston, former teachers. The minister I most wanted to be there was Charlie Bain, my probationary Superintendent and I was succeeding in office Charlie's son, Des Bain - a friend from the Edgehill College days and my Groomsman!

The chancel area of Rosemary Presbyterian Church was a large open space, allowing us plenty of room for the movements of the simple ceremony of Installation, my close friend Winston Graham was Secretary of Conference, my sisters-in-law, Violet

McElhinney and Elizabeth Harron (who had embroidered it), placed my scarf over my shoulders and my Installation Address was the speech of my life!

The Conference Sessions were in Cavehill Methodist Church, of which I was Superintendent Minister with Joanmount only a mile away, so I really felt at home in the Conference Chair. A great advantage of Conference meeting on my local patch was that I went home to my own bed each night!!

Once Conference is over, the Presidential Year begins. I said at the time that it was a bit like a woman's experience after marriage - you have to get used to your new name. I was now 'Mr. President' almost everywhere I went. I found it slightly odd when the local minister said; "The President will now dedicate the two tables," that I was the one to step forward and say the prayer! But my instincts soon became attuned to my role.

There are highly confidential matters that the President has to deal with, helped by an Advisory Committee, but the final decision has to be the President's alone - sometimes a lonely feeling with only God for company.

The vast majority of a Presidential Year is sheer joy and delight and so it proved to be for Phyllis and me. Phyllis decided to take unpaid leave from her nursing work to travel with me, so she was my driver and general organiser all the way and we both appreciated all the welcome and hospitality so freely given to us everywhere.

We went to the British Methodist Conference in Edinburgh and greatly enjoyed that experience.

Next to Australia to attend, on behalf of the British and Irish Conferences, the Triennial Assembly of the Uniting Church in Australia, in Brisbane. We found the country pleasant and easy to visit, with the friendly and welcoming culture of the people and the warm climate of Queensland and New South Wales - even in July, the Australian Winter. We were taken to see excellent work at churches, schools, a major hospital and social work projects.

The Agenda of the Assembly was almost totally dominated by the subject of human sexuality, with the liberal lobby having gained the upper hand and those with a more traditional view feeling disaffected. The whole week was somewhat painful to behold, with reports of many ministers and entire congregations leaving a denomination created in the 1970's to unite divergent theologies and traditions - Presbyterians, Congregationalists and Methodists.

Cromwell College, Brisbane where we boarded for the Assembly of Uniting Church Australia

It was hard to avoid the impression that the Uniting Church was dividing very sharply, and even bitterly.

I was selected as one of the overseas visitors to address the Assembly and my contribution went roughly as follows:

"In my homeland we have a world-famous political and religious leader who has always said 'No' to every suggested solution and we are now working hard to persuade him to say 'Yes.' It strikes me that you are, in the main, Liberal Protestants who find it hard to say 'No.'. It seems to me that the bigot never says 'Yes', and the Liberal never says 'No.' I would only suggest that there may come a time when you will have to say 'No' to something."

Wesley Central Mission in downtown Brisbane where I preached on Sunday 9th. July, 2006

I was delighted to meet Professor James Haire, whose father, Professor Jimmy Haire had taught me Theology in Belfast. He told me that the entire Assembly was about sexuality and he was right. Even the subject of the Church Pension Fund was about it - as so many ministers were leaving and wanted to know where they stood, over their superannuation accounts.

On a happier note, we met the Rev. Eric Lawson and his wife Ruth and our continued friendship led to their coming to work with us in the Methodist Church in Ireland - first in North Donegal and then later in Greenisland. The Rev. Brian Whitlock was another very willing host and tour guide for a few days, and his wife June an ideal hostess. They left us at the home of Phyllis' cousin in Brisbane, Richard Crone and his wife Sheelagh. We spent one night with them and Richard left us to the Airport for our onward flight to South Korea.

We were to attend the World Methodist Council and Conference in Seoul. We landed at Inchon Airport at a time of torrential rain and extensive flooding, and we could see the effects of it on our way by bus into the city. We had a note in Korean which was supposed to take us to our destination and I thought we were going to a Bus Station where one could seek direction according to the details on the note. But the bus driver stopped at the kerbside of a wide arterial road in the city centre and left us there with our baggage! I approached several passers-by with the note from London, they were all very polite and kindly but knew no English and none could make sense of the note.

I decided then to try to flag down a passing taxi, and after a while I succeeded. We got in and gave the driver the note - over which he frowned for about two minutes and then we were off. We came to a Bank Building, where the security man took me inside and tried to ring a telephone number on the note without success. At last the taxi man stopped at a small shop closing up for the night and the shopkeeper pointed to an uphill alleyway opposite his place of business. Driving up there we came to a Christian Hostel. It was the right place and I got the long suffering taxi man paid, discovering that he had great difficulty in walking.

Our troubles were not quite over yet! Nobody spoke English apart from the word 'Tomorrow' - we were not expected until the next day and were taken to a room full of somebody else's baggage. There we sat staring at each other and trying to figure out what on earth was going on. In about half-an-hour someone came and took us to a hastily prepared room and we settled ourselves as best we could, totally exhausted.

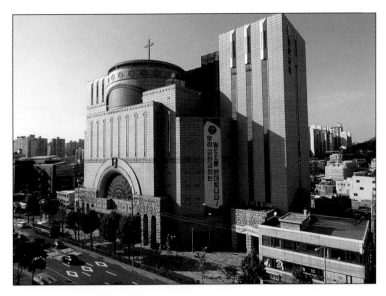

Kumnan Methodist Church, Seoul, Korea - venue of World Methodist Conference 2006

Rev.Eric & Mrs. Ruth Lawson

With the ladies in my life to mark my 60th!

Phyllis & I with Rev. Dr. Stanley & Mrs. Frances McQuade at Newcastle Methodist Church

Dedication of the new Carnalea Methodist Church October 2006

Next morning there was a note under our door from the Rev. Dr. Donghwan Kim, who soon took us under his expert wing and all was then well. Oh the adventures of foreign travel!

The rest of the British and Irish Delegates started to arrive that day and life took on a new normality. As the only breakfast available at the Student Hostel was uncooked cabbage and carrots etc., we were taken by Dong out to cafes each morning. Dong was a Korean Methodist Minister serving in England and an ideal host for us all.

Our Secretary of Conference, Winston Graham and I were the Irish Conference's representatives at the World Methodist Council - much like a Methodist Conference anywhere in format. The most interesting item of business for me was the somewhat controversial application of the Bahamas Conference - those who had split with the M.C.C.A. - to join the world body. I knew many who were there from both sides of that sad dispute, compounded with politics, race, seizure of property and legal hostility. The salient point was that, despite the opposition of the Caribbean and British Conferences, the Bahamas Conference was admitted.

The World Methodist Council is an executive body with a business agenda and it is followed directly by the World Methodist Conference which is a large-scale, American-dominated convention with lots of oratory and applause. Like the proverbial curate's egg, it was good in parts. I felt proud that Ireland could contribute so much. Gillian Kingston was Conference Arrangements Secretary and so very effective in the running of the whole programme. One of the main keynote speakers was the Rev. Dr. Heather Morris, who acquitted herself with her usual excellence. Heather was nervous before she spoke and I said a prayer with her in the midst of the loud praise being played and sung in the auditorium - God always hears and it was a truly powerful address.

Michael King of the World Church Office in London was great company and we from Britain and Ireland went out to local restaurants a few times. Linguistic and menu puzzlements sometimes resulted in unfamiliar dishes as we sat on very low seating at a long table only six inches from the floor. On one occasion we were brought a starter that looked like meadow grass. Winston Graham, sitting next to me, gave me one of his unique funny looks and said: "You always liked that song, the green, green grass of home, didn't you?" Nobody has a sense of humour remotely like Winston!

We met quite a few friends from decades before, among them Rev. Dr. J.T. Seymour and Rev. Dr. Emmette Weir, both of whom had helped to ordain me in the Bahamas in 1976.

Back home to the routine duties of such a year, visiting churches on Sundays, dedicating renovated properties and items of furniture - and one new church, Carnalea in Bangor.

The meetings with the Irish Church leaders were interesting and stimulating. Dr. David Clarke was the Presbyterian Moderator and I much admired his leadership qualities. Archbishop (later Cardinal) Sean Brady was always gracious, wise and good company. Archbishop Robin Eames was a truly outstanding Church Leader and I was a participant in a farewell event for his retirement from office, at the turn of the calendar year 06/07. In the course of all this I took part in a service in Armagh Cathedral with the then Archbishop of Canterbury Rowan Williams - I try to avoid name-dropping but sometimes I can't help myself! There was also the Dinner in the State Dining Room of Hillsborough Castle, hosted by the Secretary of State, Peter Haine, to mark Robin's retirement. I sat in deep conversation with one Gerry Adams!!!

There are numerous chit-chat social occasions mixed into such a period of office, government departments putting on promotional events to launch some new programme etc. Around the Christmas season, invitations to receptions here and there, fine if your diary permits you to attend, but I found it difficult at times to get substitutes to go in my place if I could not attend. To have to tell some polite stranger that you are there because the President couldn't come is not something a busy colleague will be eager to do!

Essential administration and correspondence had to be fitted into every spare half hour - Phyllis being my personal assistant and organiser behind the scenes. The variety of people, places and occasions was great, the calendar was full and anything to do with our personal or family affairs had to be fitted in as best we could. My surprise 60th. Birthday Dinner in Castlewellan during the Castlewellan Holiday Week, with my mother, sisters Charlotte and Irene and all our grandchildren present, was a wonderful moment to enjoy.

Urgent matters kept popping up from nowhere, such as a letter to support a visa application for a student going to the U.S.A., to recommend someone for a Royal

Honour, or legal papers to be signed to sell property, newspaper articles to be written on current affairs, or a T.V. recording crew coming to the Manse to take footage for a news programme.

A delegation of Lay Leaders would ask to meet the President as they were so unhappy about the proposed new minister for their Circuit. My son Andrew, home on holiday from Barcelona where he lives, had to listen, until I got home, to an irate person complaining about a local grave dispute. A group of politicians from Iraq had to be engaged with over sectarianism, to learn lessons that would help them normalise affairs at home. We formed a panel from the main Churches in Ireland for this and I found myself the leading person as I was the only denominational head there. Phyllis and I sat with the Mayors of Belfast, Londonderry, Dublin and Cork for informative conversations.

One Sunday evening, after long journeys and inspiring services, I was feeling tired and ready for bed when I got a 'phone call insisting that I should sack one of our ministers for addressing four hundred young people and describing Jesus as a failure! As I did not possess the power to sack the minister even if he had become a heretic, I listened patiently for long enough to give the caller the satisfaction that she had gone right to the top with her complaint!

Phyllis' father, Pop Harron, decided to reside in the Care Home to which he had been going for periods of respite when we were on holidays etc. This left Phyllis free to travel with me around Ireland and beyond. His health was declining and he died in Whiteabbey Hospital. Fortunately we were both at home and both with him as he quietly passed away whilst I was saying the Aaronic Blessing. Phyllis' aunt Ettie, so dear to our hearts as well, died on the evening of Pop's Funeral Day. With all the demands and travel we were grateful to be at home just at the right time.

Mum was still in Ardnagesson and any time I had appointments in the North West we stayed there and so I was able to visit my old home as often as in any year. I was invited by David Henderson, the Captain of 1st. Donegal Boys' Brigade Company, to be the Inspecting Officer at their Annual Display in Spring 2007 - the one out of all my engagements that I appreciated most.

Canon Raymond Fox also had me with him to preach at Laghey Parish Church, with so many family connections including our family grave, and I met my

With Revs Margaret Ferguson & Jim Rea at Shankill Methodist

With Rev. Dr. Sam Kobia, General Secretary of World Council of Churches & Archbishop Harper of Armagh May 2007

With my ordaining President, Rev. Dr. Claude Cadogan, Kingston, Jamaica 2007

Rev. Steve Wilde, with Clarence the frog & Phyllis at Cliff College

With my classmate from 1967, Bob Fairbeard, at Cliff

former Sunday School Teacher, Hannah Wilson. I spoke at a Circuit Rally in Donegal Methodist Church that same evening where I had been confirmed in membership and where I had devoted my unworthy life to Christ.

Two events near the end of my Presidency stand out in my mind:

The M.C.C.A. Conference was celebrating forty years as an autonomous Church in 2007, and the search was on for a suitable representative of British and Irish Methodism to attend. As I had been ordained by that Conference, the lot fell on me, so Phyllis and I were off to Jamaica for five days to help celebrate that landmark in Caribbean Methodist history. The Connexional President was Rev. Dr. George Mulraine, and the Secretary of Conference, the Rev. Otto Wade - whom I had helped to ordain in the Turks Islands in the 1970's. Personal highlights were meeting the Rev. Dr. Claude Cadogan who had presided at my ordination, and hearing a brilliant Lecture on West Indian history by the Rev. Dr. Bill Watty.

The other significant moment for me was our visit to Cliff College for the 124th. Anniversary. I was appointed to preach at one of the main services in the Cliff Hall Tent and later in the College Chapel and to preside at Communion on the Tuesday morning before the last of the crowd left. The big consideration for me was that it was exactly forty years since I was in my first Term at Cliff, hoping to

Preaching at Cliff Festival 2007, with Rev. Dr. Martyn Atkins,
(seated) College Principal & President Designate of the British Conference

Rev. Dr. Stephen & Mrs. Marlene Skuce

make the essential academic progress to candidate for the ministry. One of our Irish ministers, the Rev. Dr. Stephen Skuce and his family were so much part of the Cliff community and it was all a great pleasure.

Marlene Skuce left us to Manchester Airport for the journey home. There was enough time to spare for me to sit at a cafe table and write the notes for my final speech as President at the Cork Conference soon to come.

I handed the Presidential Bible to the Rev. Roy Cooper, another friend from Edgehill College days, and I returned to North Belfast to resume my calling as an ordinary minister.

(L to R) Rev. Desmond Bain, myself, Rev. Roy Cooper. We occupied the 'nursery' bedroom at Edgehill 1969 & by 2007 were successive Presidents of the Methodist Church in Ireland

THE TALE END OF THE PRESIDENCY

One day in the Spring of 2007, I got a 'phone call from someone at the Democratic Unionist Party to say that Dr. Paisley wanted me to bring a delegation from the Methodist Church to see him, to consult over whether or not to go into a power-sharing government with Sinn Fein. With only a few days notice we went, and my companions all spoke before me as I wanted to have the final say myself. As the others spoke, I sat there in a grand committee room in Stormont, looking at Ian Paisley. Half a century before, as a youngster in the Republic of Ireland, I used to think that he was a crazy fanatic. Statesmanship was written all over him now. Now he was sitting where he had always wanted to be, and we, the moderate Methodists whom he had so often pilloried, were encouraging him to form the cross-community Executive and become First Minister. What a turnaround! If there was only one man in the world who knew how to get there, that man was Ian Paisley.

He was First Minister of Northern Ireland for one year, but not before he had stirred the cauldron of Ulster's tragic sectarian mix for a lifetime. John F. Kennedy once said that "those who make peaceful revolution impossible make violent revolution inevitable." May Ian Paisley rest in peace.

JOANMOUNT

When the Presidential Year was over, I took a six-week break to rest and recover from it - and for a fortnight of that time Phyllis and I had a lovely holiday in Guernsey and Sark. I started back to work in Joanmount on 1st. August 2007 - knowing that if God would spare me, I had five years to run in the full work of the ministry. Having served in the Methodist itinerant system for so long, that seemed like a sufficiently long period during which to achieve something in pastoral and missionary terms.

Although I had already been in Joanmount for my year as President-designate, I felt that this was the moment when I was properly starting my pastorate there and the

Joanmount Methodist Church

Stewards and Leaders were sitting with a plan of action on the table, waiting for me to walk in! They certainly had not been lazy, waiting for me to return with some ideas.

There had been some discussion of the possibility of running the 'Church, Community and Change' programme in Joanmount before I left for the Presidency and they were ready to go with that, having done the initial planning. It was a social research and community action exercise provided by Tearfund and our facilitator was the Rev. Fred Vincent. The whole system worked very well for us, ran for eighteen months and led to the start of our 'First Tuesday (of the month) Lunch + for the 50 +.'

The lunch and accompanying entertainment, speaker or information sharing event, proved to be a positive cross-community success. We ran it under the umbrella of 'Joanmount Open Door' - the social outreach arm of the church which had been operating for years before my time. Wilson Lambe, Gerry Dougherty, Alan Taggart, Daphne Lambe and Wesley Doak, along with many others, were very effective in the running of the whole Open Door venture, with its Pre-school Playgroup, Carer and Toddler Group and Seniors' Friendship Club as the main activities. This was all in addition to the normal congregational life of Joanmount, which had the usual youth and women's organisations and it made for a full and exciting pastoral life. There was a tedious side to it all - the form-filling administration to apply for grants, cash-flow difficulties especially when wages have to be paid promptly and the general responsibility for supervision, management and funding, all of which go with the territory of social enterprise.

My team of fellow-workers, all volunteers apart from the two preschool teachers, were so active and supportive that I never felt unduly burdened.

Ms. Keeva Watson, Youth Pastor

My last word to the Joanmount Church Council before bowing out for the Presidential year in 2006 was that I thought they should consider getting a Youth Pastor for the Church. Somewhat to my surprise, when I returned in 2007 they were ready to roll on this project too. The groundwork had been laid to get grants and funds from our Irish Methodist Home Mission Fund, the Rank Trust and other sources to employ Miss Keeva Watson as Youth Pastor. Keeva was a pleasure to work with and a real success in her ministry among our young people. She was with us for four years - the last year being shared with Cavehill Methodist Church and she then worked part-time in Cavehill alone whilst engaging in a study programme. I have usually been fortunate in those who have worked with me and I certainly was when Keeva was in Joanmount and Cavehill. On my last two Easter Sundays I confirmed new young members and Keeva had been instrumental in helping each one of them on their way to faith and church membership.

I was keen to start a Caribbean Candlelight Service on an ecumenical basis in Joanmount. This is a liturgy whereby seven candles are lit after the reading of each of seven Scripture Lessons and I had used it often before, both in the West Indies and after returning to Ireland.

So, from 2007 onwards, on the third Sunday of Advent in the evening, we met in Joanmount Methodist Church for our United Community Candlelight Service. It brought the Catholic and Protestant Churches together for an evening of positive worship and fellowship. Political leaders from both sides of our community attended, including the Lord Mayor of Belfast when Councillor Pat Convery held that office.

My mother had been in failing health for many years and increasingly her life became a struggle, especially after my father died and she was alone in the old farmhouse where she was born. She had seldom been away from that farm, and the number of nights she slept elsewhere had been few. Such is the way of farming life that you have to stay with it and farming was the life she knew and loved. In the latter years Charlotte and Irene took on more and more care and work, such as the laundry. Olive Corrigan was a very good 'home-help' for many years.

By the Spring of 2009, the point was reached when the difficult decision to remove mum to Irene's home had to be made. We gathered for what we felt to be a significant Exodus in our family life, but to our astonishment, such was the decline in her emotional life, that she left Ardnagesson without the sentiment and sore crying that was expected! Going back to when Charlotte and I were at college and all over the years, mum wept bitterly every time we left after a break at home. In the last year or two of her life that tendency towards emotional brokenness had all gone. One day she said to me, "I have lost my feelings." She was aware of the change and it was a true saving grace. The care Irene and Charlotte gave to our mother during her last few months is beyond any words of appreciation or praise I could ever write or say. Mum passed away on a Sunday morning and my Circuit Steward, Daphne Lambe was away on holiday so I

With Joanmount leaders

With Bishop Harold Millar & fellow Canons at St. Anne's Cathedral

decided to lead the Joanmount morning service as usual and Phyllis and I went to Irene's at Convoy straight from church. Our dear friend, Ian Henderson joined us there to plan the Funeral - which was a service of thanksgiving for a wonderful Mother. I knew that emotion would not permit me to refer to my two sisters and their dedication to our mother so Ian said it for me.

After that, I felt that the old home at Ardnagesson was derelict and dead and my focus was now in South-East Antrim with my children and grandchildren.

In my last year at Joanmount, we managed to re-build the main entrance of the church and create a light catering kitchen and welcome area to replace the dilapidated structure from 1964. I was delighted with the whole project, and particularly that my good friend, the Rev. Ian Henderson was the President who dedicated it to the Glory of God.

Daphne Lambe was a very helpful and supportive Circuit Steward and Albert Morton the most effective pastoral worker I ever knew.

Throughout these seven years I was Superintendent of Cavehill and the Rev. Heather Bell and then the Rev. Tom Clarke were ideal people to work with.

The Belfast District once again called upon me to be District Superintendent for my last two years before retirement. By the grace of God I sought to rise yet again to the committee attendance and all that goes with such an office.

I had a steady and stimulating day's work in Joanmount. Occasionally there were very long days or unusually busy weeks as is usual in pastoral ministry - when a death occurs in the midst of an already full diary for example, but life would always return to a liveable normality. The Stewards and Leaders were encouraging and the people easy to serve and always appreciative of my efforts. Just as at Mountpottinger, there was a total absence of unreasonable criticism and selfish demands.

St. Annes Cathedral installed me as an Ecumenical Canon - though fortunately that only meant dressing up, looking the part and processing to the Canons' Stalls as occasion required.

Mark and Cathy had by now, been blessed with Marianne and Robert and Debbie with Olivia, and our life's experience continued to be enriched by our grandchildren.

The bungalow intended for our retirement home was on rent for a few years and the work to prepare it for our residence started in February 2012 - the year of my 'sitting-down' after forty years in the work. Mark was our contractor and the tradesmen who did the work were excellent. It meant that these last few months before and after my retirement were very hectic for Phyllis and for me.

I was sixty-six on my birthday in July and knew that this was the right time to go. Departure from any pastoral station is emotional and especially so when it is one's last station, but due to the plans laid for the first year of my retirement, I was spared the shedding of tears over the question; "What am I going to do with myself now?"

THE TALE END OF JOANMOUNT

After forty years in the ministry in different parts of the world, I thought I had seen just about everything that can take place at funerals. It was close to my retirement date when I had one in North Belfast and a couple of new features popped up. The deceased had reposed at home, and when I went to lead departure devotions at the house on the morning of the funeral, I noticed that the coffin was draped in the Union Flag.

On my way to the church I decided that if the flag was still on as the remains were brought into the sanctuary, I would let it pass. At the church entrance one of the undertakers approached me about the matter and I simply said, "It's the flag of the country and we have it up on a pole at the Communion Rail every year on Remembrance Sunday, so it's ok."

I knew that the late member was a strong Loyalist but one of my Stewards informed me that his nephew, a Catholic Priest was in attendance. This fact I only learnt after the church service.

The wonders and surprises were not all over yet! At the Crematorium Church in Roselawn, the same undertaker approached me again with a compact disk in his

126

hand. The disk contained a recording of 'The Sash My Father Wore' and it was the dying wish of the deceased that it should be played as the catafalque bearing his coffin descended out of the sight of his family and friends. I was at a loss to know what to do as the descent of the remains is the solemn moment when the minister reads the Committal. The undertaker and I stared at each other in bewilderment and then Tom, the Warden of the Crematorium Church stepped up and suggested a solution based on his previous experience of such dilemmas. He put it to me that I should read the entire liturgy, including the Benediction, before pressing the button to trigger the descent. Then the C.D. could be played as requested, as the coffin went down. Although I did feel somewhat self-conscious during the last phase of the proceedings, all was well.

As I drove through Belfast on my way home, my thoughts were; Thank God for people like Tom, men of experience who can come up with a way out of such nightmares, because what would it have been like for me to be saying "Forasmuch as it has pleased Almighty God......" to the tones of "It is old, but it is beautiful and its colours they are fine," "......to take to Himself the soul of our dear brother here departed...." "...it was worn at Derry, Augherim, Enniskillen and the Boyne." Thank God indeed for those who have learnt from experience.

JAMAICA

The famous Bishop Lancelot Andrews once said; "Thank God for the call, the recall and many calls besides." It resonates with me due to a sense of recall to the Caribbean which grew in my mind during the last ten years before I retired. It is indeed right and necessary to question and test such a feeling of guidance. Is it really of God or am I simply being foolhardy and refusing to recognise my ageing limitations? My mother was the last parent Phyllis and I had left in this life and I knew that it would be wrong for me to go back overseas leaving my two sisters to continue caring for her with no help from me after my retirement. Mother had died three years before I was due to retire and the way seemed to be clear on the family front. When we first went abroad in our twenties, we thought much about our grandparents - would they

Duncan's, our eleventh and last Manse

still be around when we came home? Some of them were indeed gone. Now, going away again in our sixties, our emotional focus tended to be on our grandchildren for we knew we would miss them. But we were both in reasonably good health, so a return to the Caribbean seemed like an avenue worth exploring.

Phyllis and I went to the Methodists for World Mission Conference at Swanwick in Derbyshire in June 2011. We met the main speaker, Rev. Dr. George Mulraine, President of the Connexional Conference, of the Methodist Church in the Caribbean and the Americas. George and I are the same age and we were both ordained in the same year in the M.C.C.A.; he is a true gentleman and genuine scholar, talented in so many ways, especially in music and theology. When I confirmed to George that I could offer to go for the stationing year 2012/2013 to work as a senior assistant with a Superintendent, he simply said that they would be delighted to have me back and that the most likely place was Jamaica. We knew immediately that the door was open and soon we were in e-mail contact with the Rev. Everald Galbraith, President of the Jamaica District. I explained that I could give a year of part-time service in exchange for a manse with the local expenses of the work being met, without a stipend in the ordinary sense as I would be on pension in Ireland. In early February 2012, Everald informed me that the District Conference had drafted me for the Superintendency of the Duncan's Circuit! I was offering to help and this was the help I was being asked to give, so I decided to go and do my best.

At my retirement Conference in Enniskillen in June 2012, the Very Rev. Dr. John Dunlop of the Presbyterian Church, who knows Jamaica well, told me publicly that either I was fully fit and able for it or I was mad! There were a few moments during our time in Jamaica when I did ask myself whether I was fit for all this or mad to undertake it - but those instances were rare. It was very much a positive experience for Phyllis, and for me to return to a region of the world we love so much. The people are the descendants of the survivors of one of history's worst mass cruelties and evils - Caribbean / American slavery. To me the amazing thing is that generally speaking they are so good-hearted, gracious and kind.

The Duncan's Circuit in the Parish (County) of Trelawny, is mainly a hills and mountains territory, with six churches and seven schools and the main local industry is farming. Goats and dogs wander freely everywhere, some cattle and a few sheep, pigs and chickens. Horses, mules and donkeys are commonly used as pack carriers as much of the arable cropping is done in the rich soil on the steep hillsides. Yam and banana are the main local crops, but papaya, citrus and mango are to be found as well, and some breadfruit. Ginger and coffee are grown elsewhere on the island. We had one of the few surviving sugar factories, with quite extensive cane fields to supply it with raw material. Most of the sugar cane is harvested by heavy machinery. The sugar industry is only a shadow of its former self, long gone are the British colonial days when it used to be said that "sugar is king in Jamaica" - which meant that it was then the dominant sector of the economy.

A few days before we left for Jamaica, Phyllis and I were in our local supermarket and there on the fruit display were papayas from Jamaica. I said; "Let's buy a couple of those, for in another week or so, I might be preaching to the farmers who grow them." The last thing I would have thought was that I would be one of the farmers myself! The Manse yard had around ten good papaya trees - and the great boon is that they bear fruit for most of the year. We also had passion fruit, pomegranates, a local type of cherries and even one pineapple!

Duncan's Methodist Church as seen from Manse

The Manse was a 1960's bungalow on the rocky hill above our Duncans Church, basic but perfectly adequate, the eleventh and last manse we would occupy. We had good and helpful neighbours and very supportive Stewards, Leaders and church members. A welcoming party of good and generous people had prepared food for our arrival in the same way as would happen anywhere in church life. The next day we were shopping and sweating with the locals in the one supermarket in town and buying from the stalls our initial supply of fruit and veg. We soon got to know the stall holders in the open square and those who ran small shops and cafes.

Duncans is just off the North Coast Highway - the tourist strip of that part of the

Local agricultural show

Passion fruit flower in Manse garden

Pineapple growing in Manse garden

Paypaya fruit in Manse garden

Ackee tree in Manse garden.

A farmer on his way to his field with donkey & foal.

The Northern Irish have been here before!

With newborn goat from local herd

Ulster Spring Methodist Church!

A branch of growing bananas

island - and sometimes tourists did appear in the town, so at first those who didn't see us in church took us for holidaymakers. But that soon changed as we tried to throw in our lot with the people as best we could. A plain wooden pectoral cross marked me out as a Minister during the week and those of every church or none were very friendly and welcoming. We bought our potatoes and vegetables from the open market and our honey from a local Rasta Man, Tiger by nickname - all locally produced, fresh and of high quality.

The Third World has all the amenities of modern life, but in a less efficient way than the First World economy. Things tend to be old and worn out, repaired and patched up. This applies to every utility and convenience of life - roads, cars, electricity, water, telephone, internet and television. As everyone has to contend with the same shortcomings, everybody understands and people will always try to help you. Every time I had a flat wheel, a couple of willing helpers jumped out of nowhere to change it for me! Motor mechanics are utterly adept at keeping cars on the road for twenty or thirty years.

The poor have hardly any of the facilities mentioned above; many live in shacks or half-built houses with no legal entitlement to the ground they call home. Separate kitchens or outdoor cooking-places are common, and shack toilets of rusted corrugated iron nailed to rotting sticks - with things like the soles of old running shoes for hinges on the door and a pit latrine. Right next door may be the luxury home of a 'returnee' family, (large, lordly and ostentatious), with plenty of finance from decades of working in England or North America. The back streets of any town tend to be rocky tracks, scarcely accessible to an ordinary car, and many of the returnees grand homes have been built along these very rough lanes.

With such economic contrasts it is not surprising that crime - much of it violent and murderous - occurs daily at a high level. Tragically sometimes it involves children as totally innocent victims when adults take vengeance in the most convenient way. Most of the crime takes place in the 'gang warfare' and drugs-related scene, with police shootings and the fatal shooting of business people on their way to the bank etc. A variety of lines of organised crime abound in Jamaica, much of it with an international dimension. When we were there 'the Lottery Scam' was operated on an industrial scale and had tarnished the reputation of the country overseas in a serious way. The method was to 'phone mainly older people in North America and tell them that they had won the Jamaica National Lottery.

If they fell for it and disclosed their banking codes, they were relieved of all their money. The matter was serious enough for a Congressional Enquiry to be held in Washington D.C. into the Jamaica Lottery Scam, with numerous families testifying to the financial ruin of their parents, in old age. There was at that time a big push to crack down on this, with armed police raids on the fortified houses used for the Scam.

While we were aware of many a calamity caused by crime, or as the result of reckless driving on the roads, Phyllis and I had a positive and happy experience of Jamaica. One lady I met greeted me with a broad intelligent sort of smile and said: "Welcome to Jamaica, when we are good we are very good, and when we are bad we are very bad!" It is no great surprise that, working in the Church, we met the very good ones - no doubt if I had been working with the police I would have met the very bad ones.

My core duty was to preach and administer Communion in two of our six churches on each of the first three Sundays of the month. This gave all of our churches monthly Communion and I also went during the week with the Lord's Supper - and a car load of Communion Stewards - to the homes of those no longer able to attend church. I felt that these Home Communions were the most important duty of all, and what God had brought me back to the Caribbean to do more than anything else.

On Sundays I wore the white preaching gown I was ordained in and a scarf in the seasonal colour. We followed the printed liturgy on most occasions at the main acts of worship and there were four readings at each service as laid out in the Revised Common Lectionary. Services usually lasted between two and three hours, nothing was rushed and there was a relaxed sense of peace at prayer. Greetings were elaborated upon at length by the Duty Steward - birthdays, births, marriages and deaths, those absent and those back after illness and the remotest connections and relatives. This part of the services was full of good humour; one Sunday the Steward forgot her glasses, I gave her mine and she could see - you can be sure that lightened the atmosphere with plenty of laughter!

On the fourth or fifth Sundays of the month, we fitted in services of a special nature - for Men's Fellowships, Women's Groups, or Harvest Thanksgiving (usually in February or March). Baptisms, both of children and adults, were fairly frequent.

The custom of gathering all the children and young people at the Communion Rail for a prayer of blessing I thought was meaningful and lovely.

134

School Assemblies normally gathered outside in the playground and I greatly enjoyed them. At first the children looked at us as if we had come from another planet - as they hardly ever saw a white person in some of the villages. Soon we could hardly get out of the car on arrival, the boys pushing to my side to carry my briefcase and the girls all wanting to hug Phyllis.

I had Circuit Administration and general pastoral work to do, just like a Minister in any pastoral charge. People needed references for jobs, to open a bank account, or even in one case to apply for a firearm certificate! We had to keep track of the M.M.S.(Ireland) Grant made to us to enable this whole project, Phyllis being the book-keeper and general organiser. We also had to decide how carefully to spend money entrusted to us for charitable purposes in Jamaica, by generous friends at home.

The local ecumenical body to which I belonged was the Northern Trelawny Ministers' Fraternal and at my first meeting I became aware of the crying needs of the Granville Girls' Refuge. The facility houses around ninety young women at any time, all of whom are victims of abuse and some of whom are 'wards of the state' or juvenile prisoners. The accommodation is overcrowded and the big effort was to complete a shell building in the grounds to provide a dedicated counselling and therapy space. There was on the staff a highly-trained and excellent psychotherapist who lacked the appropriate context in which to work.

The Ministers' Fraternal had been approached about the matter, but the project had never got off the ground. Phyllis and I were asked if we could help, and Phyllis made the need known to the all-Ireland officers of Methodist Women in Ireland -who made a generous donation from their funds. Meanwhile, money was coming from other international sources, thus bringing the building a little further on. When our son Mark was with us, along with his family, for Easter 2013, he decided to run a double Marathon in aid of Granville. He was so well supported by business associates, friends and Greenisland Methodist Church, that the sponsorship surpassed expectations and provided enough money to complete the building. In fact all our family and friends who visited us in Duncans made generous donations to this cause. When we last saw it in March 2014, the therapy rooms were finished and equipped and men were working on the upper storey - a small apartment where a social worker who might come later in the day with a distraught girl could spend the night, or where a visiting relative from another part of the island could stay.

The female victims of abuse in Jamaica desperately need help and the sad truth is that little can be done for some of them. Most can be healed and cured by good-quality therapy. We were able to help towards the provision of an appropriate facility for such a sensitive exercise of counselling to take place.

Mrs. Gloria Viera was Senior Steward of our Duncans Church, a feisty lady in her eighties. As a social worker attached to the Courts many years ago, she became aware of the tragedy of abandoned babies and young children - usually because of some handicap. A typical emergency 'phone-call late at night would come from a duty sergeant to tell her that a baby had been left on the front steps of his police station.

She founded Westhaven Childrens' Home and all the residents have physical and or mental challenges. The government provide just about enough money to pay the staff and every other cost for food, furniture, sanitary equipment etc., must be funded from private sources. A good proportion of that money comes from within Jamaica - from generous companies, schools  and families. But all such social enterprises depend on money from outside the country. Much of the money so kindly given to Phyllis and myself for Jamaica went to Westhaven and as I write that is an ongoing effort.

My sister Charlotte Maye, came to Jamaica just before taking up office as President of Methodist Women in Ireland and she decided to make the Jamaica National Childrens' Home in Kingston her President's Project. It is a social provision of the Methodist Church modelled on the National Childrens' Home in British Methodism, and the M.W.I. money greatly enhanced the work at a time of financial crisis.

Poverty, begging and obvious human need are all too common throughout Jamaica and any little that we could do was the proverbial 'drop in the ocean' but it is better to put in a small drop than nothing at all.

136

Sugar cane displayed for sale

Sticks supporting the Yam plants whilst the tuber grows

Hill road through the parish of Trelawny

Farmer harvesting breadfruit

The hills of Trelawny - 'the Jamaican alps!'

137

Well appointed home of 'returnee' Jamaican family

class of infant or 'basic' school

Basic home of a large poor family

A Primary School outdoors

High School Assembly

Mrs. Nan Frame (widow of Rev. Sydney Frame) & Mrs. Hazel Magowan,
(widow of Rev. Tom Magowan). The Magowans were Missionaries in Jamaica.

The M.C.C.A. Crest found at almost every Methodist Church in Jamaica

I wanted to return to a Circuit in the M.C.C.A., and the door opened to Jamaica and to Duncans. Without a background in the Caribbean Region, it would have been much more difficult to understand and relate to the local situation. Culture is vitally important and varies widely throughout the world and I can think of nothing that highlights cultural contrast more than a Funeral. In Ireland 'keep it as short as you can;' in the Caribbean 'make it as long as you can.' In Ireland 'keep it quiet;' in the Caribbean 'let it be as loud as possible.'

In Ireland, the very thought of a large white hearse on its way to the grave belting out mega sound Gospel music would shock the community, but in Jamaica it is normal.

A relentless round of unforeseen duties kept popping up throughout the year and the notice of date and time always tended to be short. An example was the somewhat elaborate closing exercises of the school year in June and early July. These are 'graduation days,' with cap and gown for those leaving any school, be it nursery, primary or secondary. For each there were invited chairpersons, special speakers and of course the chaplain's prayers. As the dear chaplain was leaving after only one year, a member of staff was appointed to brag about him at length! In one case I handed in a short paragraph about myself as requested, only to sit on the day listening to a long biography. On enquiring afterwards, I discovered that Google had led the appointed teacher to the website of St. Anne's Cathedral, Belfast!

The whole Duncans Circuit was struggling financially and in every way, as it was a depleted rural situation. I greatly appreciated our Stewards, Leaders and Local Preachers - all so determined to serve the Lord with gladness, but they faced many difficulties. Our properties all had faults, some of them glaring and there was simply no money to repair them. The only hope seemed to be to get a Mission Team from America with money and workers to improve things.

Despite the ongoing struggle with negative factors, we had Baptisms - both of children and adults - and new people attending and some real signs of hope. We

Mrs. Gloria Viera, founder of Westhaven
with the first resident of the home

Donation for Westhaven from
well wishers at home

Westhaven children with carers

Westhaven

were not the first people from the North of Ireland to go to the hills of Trelawny, for one of our village churches was in Ulster Spring! It was in Ulster Spring that I had four Confirmations on our last Sunday there, a sign that the Spirit was moving among our young people.

During the year in Duncans, our District President, the Rev. Everald Galbraith came to visit us from time to time in the normal course of things, usually to stay overnight. On one occasion his wife Sherraine came with him and we had good fellowship in the Manse. It was during these visits that the subject of a definite programme of evangelism and outreach came up. The President knew that I was interested in it and he suggested that I might return to the Jamaica District as a Travelling Evangelist to help facilitate the programme. Phyllis and I reflected on this invitation and after some thought and prayer, we both felt that I should agree to go back for a three-month period - January, February and March 2014.

This outreach project was set up under the title of 'Feet on the Ground,' and its main feature was the Methodist people going out of the comfort zone of church buildings to the public space to share the Christian Message appropriately with the wider community. My role within it, for the three months, was as a visiting preacher at carefully planned Open Air Meetings, and as a lecturer on preaching at a series of Training Seminars at different venues around the island. The realisation had grown that the M.C.C.A. was in decline and if we did not re-evangelise we would perish. There was also a felt need to inspire and encourage Ministers and Lay Preachers, as unfortunately there was much to discourage them. For these seminars I worked alongside the President, repeating our input on five occasions. By the end of it, we both knew our own material and each others addresses off by heart! I preached in a different Circuit each Sunday and at twenty-six Open Air Witness events!

To fulfil this itinerary, Phyllis and I were based at an apartment integral to the home of Mrs. Bev. Watson in the suburbs of Montego Bay. However, most of the time we were residing in the homes of church members in whatever Circuit I happened to be working. We already knew the Caribbean well over many years, but we learnt more in these three months by living with our people. The food and general hospitality were simply marvellous and our lives were enriched by the Christian love shown to us everywhere.

The District President, through the relevant committees had decided that we could not just sit and watch the church decline. The motivation in the minds of

Rev. Everald Galbraith (District Bishop), myself, Rev. Otto Wade (Presiding Bishop of MCCA.)

Early morning Open Air Service in Duncan's public square

District Evangelism programme

Confirmation

I rest before preaching at an Open Air Rally

Home Communion

Training Seminar for Preachers

Memorial to a predecessor in my Circuit

143

deeply committed people to take our message out into the cities, towns and villages of Jamaica was once again growing. In the cultural and social context of that country, open air preaching was appropriate and effective in a way that it no longer is in Ireland.

When I was in the Bahamas in the 1970's evangelism was relatively easy and straightforward, and it usually took the shape of one-week Missions in our churches. It was then in that format that many people came to fresh faith in Christ, and such evangelism was a natural activity in the programme of any Methodist Circuit or local church. Since then the same secular cynicism that we have in Europe has come to affect the Caribbean. The mass media and the social media have brought these thought-forms to the region and Tourism has brought low personal morals with it. All these factors have made evangelistic outreach more difficult than it used to be. It is still possible with the momentum of spiritual power, plus the sheer human determination to go out and do it.

When we arrived in a Circuit, my programme was organised in advance; I would preach in one of the churches if I was there for a Sunday, and school assemblies were often lined up for me as well. The Teachers in school were as welcoming as the Stewards in church, the processing choirs would sing to full volume and every duty was sheer delight for me. For the Open Air Witness, we set ourselves up at a variety of venues - sometimes simply the front yard of our own Methodist Church, in a town square or shopping plaza or outside a convenience store in a residential street - all places where people naturally gather in the evening. A praise group would sing, making plenty of noise with tambourines and drums! The audience would gather and grow, testimonies would be given about various aspects of Christian living - often about passing through hard times due to illness, tragedy or poverty. We were never short of distractions, such as fighting dogs, extremely loud engines, drunk persons or delivery vehicles stopping in front of the preacher! There was never any heckling, deliberate opposition or contradiction.

After about one or even two hours of these preliminaries, I would give an informal address, keeping it as spontaneous as possible, about the saving grace of God and the Christian hope. John Wesley's way of describing such ministry "I offered them Christ," often sprang to my mind.

On every occasion, when someone else followed me with an appeal for people to begin a new walk with the Lord, there was always some response. There were those who came forward from the shadows to be met and encouraged by the local Methodist Leaders. They had literature and the means to make records and plan suitable follow-up afterwards. I often felt profoundly moved at the sight of some of the broken people who responded and in some places the minister would tell me that those who came forward had already begun to attend our local church, and a Confirmation Class would be started for them the next Sunday. The whole experience meant that I finished my full-time ministry on the sort of high note I could never have anticipated.

I am grateful to God for the re-call to the Caribbean - my second cultural and spiritual home. I am thankful to George Mulraine and Everald Galbraith and so many Caribbean colleagues, dedicated to the point of sacrifice, who welcomed me back again. They took a chance that maybe even now in my early retirement I could still make some small contribution to the work of God in Jamaica.

Phyllis gave me the same steady support she has given everywhere and all three of our sons came to visit us during our year in the Duncans Circuit. Andrew came from Barcelona for Christmas, Robert, Debbie, Lily and Olivia for the New Year and Mark, Cathy, Layla, Honor and Marianne for Easter. So our whole immediate family were able to re-connect with the Caribbean.

As we returned to Ireland in the Spring of 2014, to my sixty-eighth birthday, I knew that I must now seek a real retirement.

Thanks be to God.

The last few steps to the resting place of the deceased

The Committal

Immediately after Committal, grave is covered with concrete

The concrete is left to set

146

THE TALE OF END OF JAMAICA

At the Funeral of a very old lady, the Chief Mourner was a woman in middle-life, a granddaughter of the deceased. Women tend to have their first baby in their teens and family structures are always something of a mystery to an outsider, but this was a Chief Mourner determined not to let a significant moment pass without being seen to be centre- stage. I have a vivid recollection of the stages in that service.

The first was the Chief Mourner's very loud screaming, which delayed the start of the proceedings by half an hour, and the Church Choir could only process for the first hymn on the third attempt.

The second was her standing along with two other relatives, with beaming face, singing a Trio - a tribute to Granny.

The third was of the Chief Mourner talking happily on her mobile 'phone during my sermon. While I sought to articulate the hope of Heaven, she sat by the coffin talking merrily to someone who couldn't be there in person!

Such a service could last three hours, and then at the grave we sang hymns for well on to another hour as concrete was mixed to close the tomb-like burial place.

My private thoughts on the way home usually were, "May God indeed rest the souls of all the faithful departed."

RETIREMENT

Retirement should mean a change of pace, an easement of stress, a less cluttered diary, more time for the family and for ones personal interests. I decided not to accept a part-time pastoral job as a senior curate but to make myself available for occasional duties as required. Although my health was generally good for a man in his late sixties, deafness was increasing - for which I needed hearing aids - and I was discovering what a handicap this can be in some pastoral situations.

At our own front door AT LAST with our two elderly rescue dogs!

Andrew & Dulce at their wedding ceremony in Barcelona

Another factor of which I became aware during my ministry was that an interfering retired minister can sometimes be less than straightforwardly helpful to those who have to carry out the full range of responsibility in full-time ministry - and I dreaded the thought that I might be a problem for a younger minister. So I undertake short-term cover for colleagues on holidays, sabbaticals or off duty due to illness and I have helped with the pastoral and preaching work of circuits where the minister is in office as President.

The result has been that I preach when invited on Sundays in a variety of places and preside at Weddings, Funerals, Communion and Baptism from time to time.

We live in our own retirement bungalow in Newtownabbey, with Mark, Robert and their families living just down the

I preside at Marriage blessing of Andrew & Dulce in Greenisland Methodist

road near Greenisland. Andrew, teaching English In Barcelona married Dulce from Mexico City and their children are Owen and Ameyalli. Our visits to them and theirs to us are always enjoyable as are our frequent electronic communications.

Phyllis allowed her Nursing Registration to run out after we returned from Jamaica so we can now live a busy but not pressurised life with more time together than we have ever had before.

One of the features that attracted me to our present home was the relatively large back garden. Mark's workmen laid out permanent raised planting frames and when we returned from Jamaica in the spring of 2014, I started planting potatoes and vegetables with fruit trees and shrubs as well. Phyllis makes jams and chutneys and we eat our own garden produce every day when at home.

There were good rhubarb roots in the garden when we bought the house, our next-door neighbour gave me all her roots and a good friend at church gave me more and I now have 20 good productive rhubarb crowns around the perimeter of my vegetable plot. At one stage I had far more rhubarb than we could use, so I decided to take it to the Newtownabbey Mission on Sundays and offer it to the congregation after church. When I was explaining about it during the service I said in an 'off-the-cuff way;' "No charge, but if you want to give me 50p for Chid Care in Jamaica I'll take it!" Two results have flowed from what was an unprepared remark. Child Care in Jamaica has benefited by thousands of pounds.

We have had great banter and fun at the Mission over the rhubarb - I have sometimes said that I am more famous in Rathcoole for my rhubarb than for my preaching - a humbling thought, always good for the soul.

My garden grows!

A proud gardener with his bumper crop of apples

My ripe Victoria plums

THE TALE END OF RETIREMENT

At the conclusion of the work on our bungalow, two old living room chairs were left in the garage. I jokingly asked Mark's tradesmen not to take them away as an easy-chair is part of the gardening equipment for an old man. One day two of our granddaughters, Lily and Olivia were with us and I took a rest from working in the garden on one of these chairs. Both girls came and sat on my knee.

To make some conversation with them I said, "girls, do you ever notice when you are out and about with Grandma and me, I say to people that you are my grandchildren?" They had observed that, I then asked them if they wondered why I needed to explain that they were my grandchildren? They had never thought about that. I continued, "The reason you see, is that I am so young looking, people might think I was your father." Olivia was five years old then and with eyes wide in astonishment exclaimed; "Grandpa, how could anybody ever make that mistake, you're so old looking!"

EPILOGUE

'When as a child I laughed and wept - time crept.
When as a youth I waxed more bold - time strolled.
When I became a full grown man - time ran.
When older still I daily grew - time flew.
Soon I shall find in passing on - time gone!'
Time's Paces (Henry Twells 1823-1900)

I once heard a neighbourhoods philosopher, a local cynic, observe that heaven is the place Christians like to talk about but none of them ever seem to be in a hurry to go there!

John Wesley, in the Preface to his famous book, The forty-four Sermons, wrote: *"I am a creature of a day, passing through life as an arrow through the air. I am a spirit come from God and returning to God... a few moments hence, I am no more seen... I want to know one thing - the way to heaven; how to land safe on that happy shore."* Wesley goes on to explain how the Bible is God's roadmap to heaven.

St. Paul refers to 'what no eye has seen, nor ear heard, nor the human heart conceived, what God has prepared for those who love him.' (1 Corinthians 2 verse 9.). This describes the Christian experience of Jesus Christ as Saviour and Lord of glory in the every day, the here and now of the life of faith. A Christian is one whose ultimate home and native land is in heaven and for whom the things of earth and this life derive their true value, meaning and perspective, from the light of heaven shining on them. 'If for this life only we have hoped in Christ, we are of all people most to be pitied.' (1 Corinthians 15 verse 19.)

In the days before electric street lighting, there used to be a 'lamplighter' who went through the city streets igniting the gas lights at the top of each light pole, and it was necessary to make the round again in the morning to extinguish the lights. An old lamplighter was once asked if it was not a depressing job, starting before dawn putting out all the lights and leaving a trail of darkness behind him. "Not at all," he said, "I look ahead and there is always another light." The enquirer persisted and asked him, "But how do you feel when the last light goes out?" With a cheery smile the lamplighter replied, "Why then it's morning!"

The Christian hope is that when the lights go out in this dark world, and even our last earthly light goes out, heaven's morning will break and earths vain shadows will flee away. 'And there will be no more night; they need no light of lamp or sun, for the Lord God will be their light, and they will reign for ever and ever.' (Revelation chapter 22 verse 5.)

THE BEST IS ALWAYS YET TO BE

The Rev. Ivan McElhinney can be contacted at:

Ivan.phyllis.mcelhinney@googlemail.com

Proceeds from the sale of this book, after
costs, will go to Child Care in Jamaica.

Designed & Published by Cedric Wilson
Email: cedricwilson@live.co.uk